Baking
Cakes, Tarts and Biscuits

NAUMANN & GÖBEL

Baking

Cakes, Tarts
and Biscuits

© Naumann & Göbel Verlagsgesellschaft mbH, a subsidiary of
VEMAG Verlags- und Medien Aktiengesellschaft, Cologne
www.apollo-intermedia.de

Complete production: Naumann & Göbel Verlagsgesellschaft mbH, Cologne
Translation from German to English: Marina Benham
Printed in Germany

ISBN 3-625-10939-5

Contents

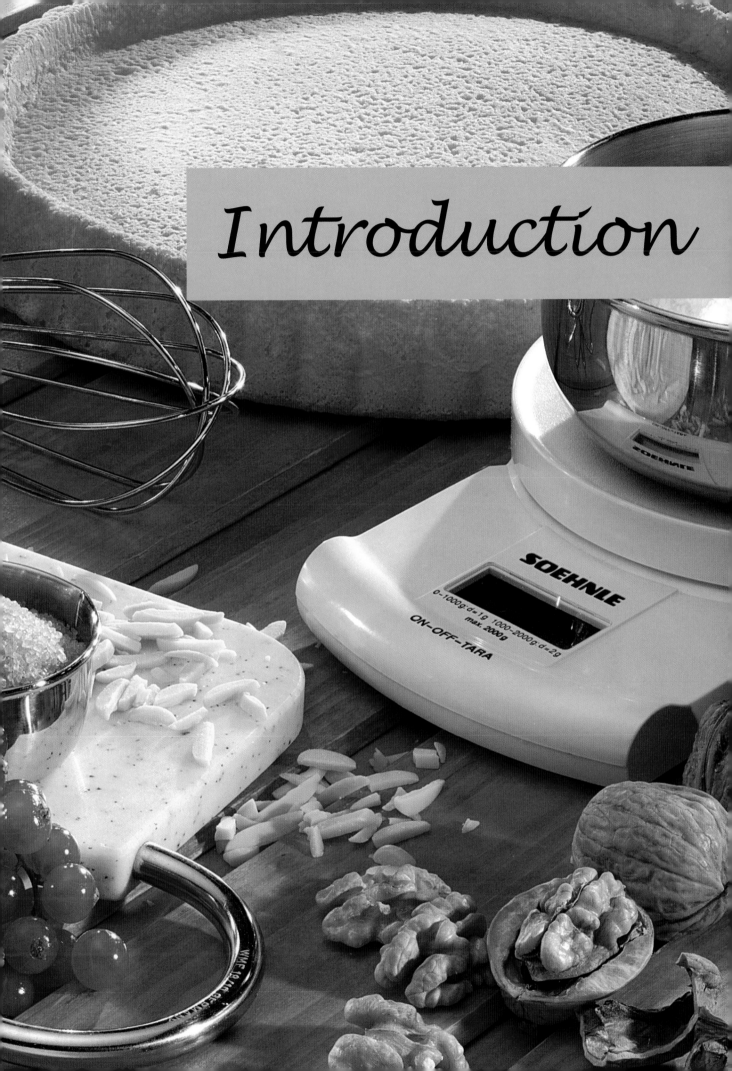

Introduction

Equipment and Utensils

Most households already have all the utensils required for baking. Here are the most important items that you will need.

A large *chopping board* made of strong, smooth wood is highly recommended. Treated well, this should last a lifetime.

Good solid *bowls*, either metal or plastic, should be in every household. And if a particular size is missing, treat yourself to a stainless steel one. While these are quite expensive, they are long-lasting and easy to clean.

Good old-fashioned *mixing spoons* generally only serve a decorative purpose in a modern household. In the main they have been replaced either by food processors or, if you are in a hurry, by hand mixers.

Even the good old *rolling pin* has a new look. The modern rolling pin is no longer big and wooden, but shiny silver or non-stick plastic.

Small *pastry rollers* with a plastic handle will shape any kind of pastry. Biscuits are easily cut out with either a smooth or a wavy pastry wheel.

Cooling racks on which cakes and pastries are left to cool, are also available, either in metal or plastic.

To cut a torte base through quickly and – more importantly – evenly, use either a sharp knife, or, better still, a *cutting wire*.

The fine wire can be adjusted to either a thin or thick setting.

Professional bakers use a rolled up piece of *baking parchment* cut off at the tip to pipe decorations on their cakes. This works beautifully if you are experienced. However, it is easier if you use a commercially available *piping bag*, as this is larger and more robust and comes with an assortment of nozzles, again in various sizes.

Despite having high tech items like a food processor or an electric whisk, you still need a good old *hand whisk*. As with the rolling pin, these come in standard and luxury models. Both serve the same purpose equally well. While the nicely rounded stainless steel version is more expensive, it is also more solid, is easy to use and easier to clean. If you've ever had the wires fall out of a whisk while cleaning it, then you'll appreciate the quality of a more expensive model.

However, there is not much choice when it comes to buying *pastry combs*. Whether they have a zigzag or a straight edge, they always serve the same purpose – to help smooth as much of the pastry mixture into the baking tin as possible. However, they are not really needed if anyone with a sweet tooth comes into the kitchen to help. The zigzag combs can also be used to decorate the tops of pastries.

Equipment and Utensils

The *palette knife* is a wide, blunt, rounded knife, and is also used for smoothing things out. This is used by cake makers mainly to trim the edges or smooth the surfaces of the cakes and tortes after these have been spread with creams and glazes.

Graters are also a must when you are baking. Lemon zest is much more aromatic if added to the pastry mixture freshly grated. But do ensure that your grater is always cleaned well, since bacteria will accumulate on deposits left behind.

You should also have *pastry brushes, spatulas* and *sieves* in varying sizes and widths.

Now let us have a look at the *scales*. Most home bakers are perfectly happy with any popular mechanical kitchen scales showing weights from 20 g/¾ oz up to 5 kg/11 lbs accurately. If you need to know the weights more exactly, you will need a more precise electronic model.

There is one more piece of equipment we recommend so that you don't have any arguments over the size of the slices:

a *cake divider*. This is a plastic template that is briefly pressed on top of the finished cake, marking where each individual piece should be cut.

Baking Tins

Equipment

The right cake tin is just as important as the perfect cake mixture or a good cooker. However, there is such a wide choice in the shops today that it is sometimes difficult to make the right decision.

We have had a look around and picked out the most popular types of tins and materials. But remember that these are only recommendations and only provide general information on the materials used.

Irrespective of what the baking tin is made from, it should only ever be cleaned using hot water and without detergent. If you soak the tin immediately after use, even the most stubborn of cake remains are easy to remove. When buying baking tins you should also check to ensure that the tin is made from a single piece, or has as few joins as possible to which pastry or cake mixture can stick. Almost all recipes recommend greasing the baking tin prior to use, and sprinkling with breadcrumbs or flour and this is a good idea. Exceptions to this are tins that have a special coating which does not need to be greased, according to the manufacturer. The cheapest baking tins are those made of tin, or black coated tin. These are light, yet robust, and are available in all the usual shapes and sizes. Black baking tins have the advantage of making the cakes brown more evenly, but they do scratch more easily. With glass or ceramic baking tins the baking process takes a little longer, but the cake or pastry bakes more evenly and is less likely to burn than in a tin made of metal. However, as these materials retain their heat for a long time, they should not be subjected to sudden temperature changes. So be careful not to place them on a cold surface after removing them from the oven.

Tins coated with non-stick surfaces are available in a range of materials and sizes. The manufacturers maintain that the special coating makes greasing unnecessary. However, if you want to make really sure that your cake comes out of the tin easily, you should still grease it lightly. This is particularly true of old baking tins where the

Baking Tins

non-stick surface has been damaged or worn away.

Tins

Let us start with the traditional spring-release tin. This is one of the most versatile cake tins around and is very popular for torte bases and fruit flans. Loaf tins in a variety of sizes should also be in every household. These tins can be used both for cakes and for making bread because they make almost pre-shaped slices.

On special occasions, such as Christmas, New Year and children's birthdays, cakes will simply

taste much better if they have been baked in a specially shaped tin, for example a star, a heart or an animal.

A popular type of tin in southern Germany and Austria is the guglhupf or Viennese ring tin. The classic guglhupf, that gave its name to this type of tin, was in fact a yeast cake mixture.

The log tin (for the prickly log) and savarin mould are decorative. The savarin mould is named after the popular French ring-shaped yeast cake.

Sponges and short crust pastries turn out best in tart or flan bases. English or American pie and French

tart tins are now available too in a wide variety of shapes, sizes and materials, with smooth or wavy edges, and with removable bases.

Quick Mixes

Quick Mixes

For 1 loaf tin
30 cm/12 in long

250 g/9 oz butter
250 g/9 oz sugar
4 eggs
250 g/9 oz plain flour
2 tsp baking powder
butter to grease the tin
flour for dusting

For the glaze:
150 g/5 oz icing sugar
2–3 tbsp lemon juice

Cake shown (without icing):
Italian Chocolate Torte (below,
recipe page 28/29)

A good quick-mix cake should be mixed really well. While food processors and mixers make life easy for us today, previously this work was done by hand, and that took time. Hence some old cookbooks state, „stir until you have said the Lord's Prayer 10–15 times". This was the time it took for the mixture to rise. Nowadays baking is much easier. And if you are in a real hurry, just put all the ingredients for a simple quick-mix cake into a bowl and use a mixer. The baking powder will make the cake rise.

Put the softened butter in a bowl.

Whisk the mixture until soft and creamy using a hand mixer.

Add ⅔ of the sugar and continue whisking until this has all dissolved.

Separate the eggs. The bowl must be clean and fat-free.

Basic Recipe

5 Add the yolks to the butter mixture and whisk in.

9 Grease a loaf tin.

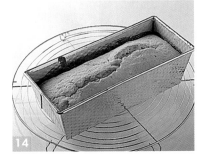

13 Test the cake to see if it is done just before the end of the baking time.

6 Mix the flour with the baking powder.

10 Dust the tin with flour.

14 Allow to cool for about 20 minutes on a wire cooling rack.

7 Gradually whisk the flour into the egg and butter mixture.

11 Pour the cake mix into the tin.

15 Turn cake out and allow to cool completely.

8 Whisk the egg whites and remaining sugar until stiff. Then stir ⅓ of this mixture into the cake mixture. Fold the rest in.

12 Level the top with a spatula.

16 Stir the icing sugar with the lemon juice until smooth, then pour over the cake.

15

Guglhupf

Makes 12 slices

250 g/9 oz butter
200 g/9 oz sugar
a pinch of salt
4 eggs
4 tbsp milk
350 g/12 oz plain flour
2 tsp baking powder
250 g/9 oz fruit in alcohol
100 g/3 ¾ oz icing sugar
walnuts (halved) to
decorate
butter for the tin

Preparation time:
1 hour 20 minutes
459 kcal/1929 kJ

1 Mix the butter with the sugar, salt, eggs and milk. Stir in the flour and baking powder, mix until smooth and creamy.

2 Preheat oven to 175 °C/340 °F/gas mark 3 ½. Drain the fruit well and chop up small. Finally stir these into the cake mixture.

3 Pour mixture into a greased Viennese ring tin, level the top and bake on the bottom shelf of the oven for about 60 minutes.

4 Allow the guglhupf to cool on a wire rack. For the icing stir the icing sugar with 4 tbsp water until smooth, then pour over the cake, and decorate with halved walnuts.

Sea Buckthorn Cake

1 Beat the butter in a bowl until smooth and creamy. Separate the eggs and mix the egg yolks and 100 g/3 ½ oz sugar with the butter. Whisk the egg whites and the remaining sugar until stiff. Stir the flour, salt and baking powder into the cake mixture, then carefully fold in the stiff egg white.

2 Remove about 6 tbsp cake mixture and mix with the honey, the sea buckthorn puree and the lemon juice. Preheat the oven to 180 °C/355 °F/gas mark 4. Stir the orange zest into the remaining cake mixture. Grease a 26 cm/10 in loaf tin and pour in a third of the main mixture.

3 Spread the buckthorn mixture on top and work spirals into the main cake mixture with a fork. Finally pour in the rest of the main mixture.

4 Bake for about 20 minutes on the middle shelf of the oven. Sprinkle with icing sugar before serving.

Makes 16 slices

150 g/5 oz softened butter

3 eggs

150 g/5 oz sugar

75 g/2 ½ oz wheat flour

75 g/2 ½ oz wholegrain wheat flour

a pinch of salt

1 tsp baking powder

1 tbsp honey

4 tbsp sea buckthorn puree

1 tbsp lemon juice

zest of one orange

butter to grease the tin

4 tbsp icing sugar

Preparation time:
approx. 35 minutes
212 kcal/912 kJ

Pumpkin and Nut Cake

Makes 16 slices

3 eggs
2–3 drops vanilla essence
400 g/14 oz sugar
200 ml/7 fl oz vegetable oil
2 tsp cinnamon
600 g/1 lb 5 oz pumpkin flesh
150 g/5 oz walnuts
500 g/1 lb 2 oz plain flour
1 tbsp baking powder
½ tsp salt
butter for the tin
icing sugar to dust

Preparation time:
1 hour 20 minutes
135 kcal/569 kJ

1 Separate the eggs. Whisk egg yolks, vanilla essence, sugar, oil and cinnamon until smooth and creamy.

2 Grate the pumpkin flesh, add to the egg mixture and stir well.

3 Grate the walnuts finely. Mix the flour, baking powder, salt and grated walnuts together and stir into the pumpkin mixture. Preheat the oven to 180 °C/355 °F/gas mark 4.

4 With an electric beater whisk the egg whites until stiff. Add to the cake mixture and fold in carefully.

5 Grease a loaf tin or spring-release tin. Pour the mixture into the tin and bake in the oven for about 60 minutes.

6 Remove the cake tin from the oven and allow it to cool in the tin for 10 minutes. Then turn the cake onto a cooling rack and allow to cool completely. Dust the pumpkin and nut cake with icing sugar before serving.

Apple Cake with Cinnamon

Makes 12 slices

100 g/3 ½ oz currants
100 g/3 ½ oz dried apple rings
5 tbsp white rum
200 g/7 oz butter
125 g/4 ½ oz sugar
2–3 drops vanilla essence
2 eggs
a pinch of salt
1 tbsp cinnamon
125 g/4 ½ oz plain flour
1 tsp baking powder
100 g/3 ½ oz ground walnuts
butter for the tin
3 tbsp candied apple rings to decorate

Preparation time:
60 minutes
320 kcal/1347 kJ

1 Wash the currants and apple rings and soak in the rum. Whisk the butter, sugar and vanilla essence until smooth and creamy, gradually adding the eggs. Whisk until the sugar has been completely dissolved.

2 Stir in the salt, cinnamon, flour, baking powder and grated walnuts. Carefully fold in the currants and apple rings. Preheat the oven to 180 °C/355 °F/gas mark 4.

3 Grease a loaf tin 20 cm/8 in long with butter and pour in the cake mixture. Bake on the middle shelf of the oven for 50 minutes.

4 Turn cake out of the tin and allow to cool. Decorate with candied apple rings.

Marble Cake with Pears

1 Beat the softened butter with 200 g/ 7 oz sugar until smooth and creamy. Gradually add the eggs. Preheat the oven to 170 °C/340 °F/gas mark 3.

2 Mix the flour with the baking powder and fold in. Remove ⅔ of the cake mixture and stir in the pear brandy. Grease a 24 cm/9–10 in spring-release cake tin and dust with flour. Pour in the cake mixture with no brandy in it.

3 Mix the cocoa with the remaining sugar and milk and stir into the remaining mixture. Pour the chocolate mixture into an icing bag with a large nozzle. Squeeze large drops of dark cake mix evenly into the pale mixture, inserting the nozzle ⅔ of the way into the pale mixture.

4 Drain the pears in a sieve, then dab dry. Arrange the pear halves on top of the cake mixture in a star pattern, with the rounded side downwards. Do not press down too firmly.

5 Bake the cake for about 60 minutes on the bottom shelf of the oven. Then allow to cool, and dust with icing sugar before serving.

Makes 12 slices

250 g/9 oz butter
220 g/8 oz sugar
4 eggs
400 g/14 oz plain flour
1 ½ tsp baking powder
2 tbsp pear brandy
butter and flour for the cake tin
50 g/1 ¾ oz cocoa powder
2–3 tbsp milk
1 tin pear halves (480 g/ 1 lb drained weight)
icing sugar to dust
butter for the tin
flour to dust the tin

Preparation time:
1 hour 35 minutes
406 kcal/1705 kJ

21

Redcurrant Torte

1 Preheat the oven to 180 °C/355 °F/ gas mark 4. Beat the butter until smooth and creamy. Gradually add the sugar, vanilla essence and eggs. Whisk until smooth and creamy. Sieve the flour, salt and baking powder.

2 Stir flour and milk into the mixture alternately. Pour the mixture into a 26 cm/ 10 in round spring-release tin and bake for about 55 minutes on the middle shelf of the oven.

3 Whisk the cream until fairly stiff. Soak the gelatine and dissolve in 3 tbsp cold water. Stir in the redcurrant liqueur, the jam, food colouring and gelatine. Fold in the cream.

4 Cut the torte right through horizontally twice. Remove the stalks from the red-currants, wash and dry them.

5 Cover each layer of the torte with ⅓ of the cream, sprinkle some redcurrants on top, then assemble the torte.

6 Spread the remaining cream and red-currants onto the top layer. Allow torte to cool and set for about 1 hour. Decorate with lemon balm and serve.

Makes 18 slices

100 g/3 ½ oz softened butter
100 g/3 ½ oz sugar
2–3 drops vanilla essence
2 eggs
175 g/6 oz plain flour
a pinch of salt
1 ½ tsp baking powder
6 tbsp milk
200 g/7 oz whipping cream
4 leaves white gelatine
a drop of redcurrant liqueur
1 tbsp redcurrant jam
a dash of red food colouring
150 g/5 oz redcurrants
lemon balm to decorate

Preparation time:
1 hour 30 minutes
(plus cooling time)
221 kcal/928 kJ

Marzipan Slices

Makes 24 slices

For the mixture:
150 g/5 oz butter
6 eggs
250 g/9 oz sugar
a pinch of salt
350 g/12 oz plain flour
1 tsp baking powder
6 tbsp milk
baking parchment

For the filling:
150 g/5 oz butter
100 g/3 ½ oz whipping cream
150 g/5 oz sugar
2–3 drops vanilla essence
200 g/7 oz marzipan
2 tbsp dark rum
400 g/14 oz flaked almonds

Preparation time:
60 minutes
430 kcal/1800 kJ

1 Preheat the oven to 200 °C/390 °F/ gas mark 6. Whisk the butter, eggs, sugar and salt until smooth and creamy. Mix the flour with the baking powder. Stir the flour and milk alternately into the butter mixture. Continue stirring until blended.

2 Spread the mixture onto a baking tray lined with baking parchment, level the top and bake for about 15 minutes.

3 Meanwhile mix the butter with the whipping cream, sugar, vanilla essence and marzipan and melt in a pan at a low temperature. Add the rum and stir in the flaked almonds.

4 Spread this mixture on top of the cake mixture. Bake for about 20 minutes on the middle shelf of the oven.

Courgette Cake

1 Prepare, wash and finely grate the courgettes. Peel the apples, remove the core and grate finely. Soak the raisins in rum and leave aside.

2 Beat the eggs in a bowl, drizzle in the sugar and whisk until frothy. Preheat oven to 180 °C/355 °F/gas mark 4.

3 Mix the flour, bicarbonate of soda, cinnamon and baking powder together and fold into the egg mixture. Add the oil a drop at a time, and stir well until the mixture is smooth. Mix the courgettes, grated apple, hazelnuts and raisins together. Stir them into the cake mixture.

4 Pour the mixture into a 26 cm/10 in or 28 cm/11 in greased spring-release tin, and bake for about 50 minutes on the middle shelf of the oven.

5 Allow cake to stand for about 10 minutes in the tin. Then remove and allow to cool completely. Insert a cocktail stick or thin knitting needle into the cake, and if this comes out clean, the cake is done. Serve with chocolate or hazelnut frosting (optional).

Makes 16 slices

2–3 courgettes (about 350 g/12 oz)

2 apples

100 g raisins

3 tbsp rum

4 eggs

250 g/9 oz sugar

450 g/1 lb plain flour

2 tsp bicarbonate of soda

2 tsp cinnamon

1 tsp baking powder

½ tsp salt

125 ml/4 ½ fl oz vegetable oil

125 g 4 ½ oz chopped hazelnuts

butter for the tin

Preparation time:
1 hour 25 minutes
83 kcal/349 kJ

Viennese Ring

Makes 16 slices

For the mixture:
250 g/9 oz butter
200 g/7 oz sugar
2–3 drops vanilla essence
4 eggs
350 g/12 oz plain flour
100 g/3 ½ oz cornflour
2 tsp baking powder
butter for the tin
flour to dust

For the filling:
½ l/9 fl oz milk
pulp of ½ vanilla pod
120 g/4 ¼ oz sugar
40 g/1 ½ oz cornflour
4 egg yolks
250 g/9 oz butter
125 g/4 ½ oz redcurrant jelly
2 tbsp pistachio nuts
16 glacé cherries

Preparation time:
1 hour 25 minutes
365 kcal/1534 kJ

1 Preheat oven to 175 °C/340 °F/gas mark 3. Beat butter, sugar, vanilla essence, eggs, flour, cornflour and baking powder into a smooth mixture. Grease a ring tin with butter and dust with flour. Pour the mixture into the cake tin and smooth the top.

2 Bake for 40 minutes on the bottom shelf of the oven. Allow the cake to cool a little, then remove from the baking tin, turn onto a cooling rack and allow to cool.

3 Make a butter cream for the filling using the milk, vanilla pulp, sugar, cornflour, egg yolk and butter. Cut cake horizontally 3 times.

4 Spread redcurrant jelly over the bottom ring. Place the second ring on top and press down slightly. Spread ¼ of the butter cream on this. Place third ring on top and also spread with ¼ of the butter cream. Place the last ring on top and cover the whole cake with the remaining butter cream.

5 Sprinkle pistachios over the whole cake. Put the remaining butter cream into a piping bag with a star nozzle and pipe small rosettes around the top of the cake. Put a glacé cherry onto each star and press in gently.

Italian

Chocolate Torte

1 Preheat the oven to 175 °C/350 °F/ gas mark 3 ½. Mix the butter, sugar, eggs, flour and baking powder until smooth and creamy. Melt the chocolate at a low temperature and stir in the Espresso coffee powder.

2 Allow chocolate mixture to cool, then stir into the torte mixture. Pour the mixture into a greased and dusted round 26 cm/10 in spring-release tin and bake for about 60 minutes on the middle shelf of the oven.

3 Stir the wine and rum into the icing sugar. While the torte is still warm, sprinkle this mixture over it and allow to cool. Remove from the baking tin and allow to cool on a rack.

4 Add sugar to the cream and whisk until stiff. Spread over the torte. Grate the chocolate very finely and sprinkle over the torte.

Makes 8 slices

300 g/10 ½ oz butter
300 g/10 ½ oz sugar
5 eggs
300 g/10 ½ oz plain flour
2 tsp baking powder
100 g/3 ½ oz plain cooking chocolate
1 tbsp Espresso coffee powder
½ l/18 fl oz white wine
3 tbsp rum
50 g/1 ¾ oz icing sugar
250 g/9 oz whipping cream
1 tbsp sugar
100 g/3 ½ oz plain cooking chocolate
butter for the tin
flour for dusting

Preparation time:
1 hour 30 minutes
445 kcal/187 kJ

Cherry Cake with Cream

Makes 12 slices

125 g/4 ½ oz butter
100 g/3 ½ oz sugar
100 g/3 ½ oz marzipan
5 eggs
3 tbsp lemon juice
150 g/5 oz plain flour
50 g/1 ¾ oz cornflour
2 tbsp baking powder
1 jar Morello cherries (460 g/1 lb drained weight)
butter to grease the tin
flour to dust the tin
150 g/5 oz thick sour cream
3 tbsp icing sugar

Preparation time:
1 hour 10 minutes
352 kcal/1479 kJ

1 Whisk the butter and sugar until creamy. Add the marzipan and whisk until blended. Stir in the three eggs, one at a time, then the lemon juice.

2 Mix the flour with the cornflour and baking powder, sieve and stir into the cake mixture, a spoon at a time. Drain the cherries well in a sieve.

3 Preheat the oven to 175 °C/345 °F/ gas mark 3 ½. Pour the cake mixture into a greased and dusted 24 cm/10 in spring-release tin. Spread the cherries evenly across the surface.

4 To make the glaze mix the sour cream with the eggs and 1 tbsp icing sugar. Spread on top of the cherries, then bake in a pre-heated oven on the bottom shelf.

5 Unfasten spring release and remove cake, and allow to cool. Dust with the remaining icing sugar.

Fig Cake

Makes 12 slices

3 eggs
100 g/3 ½ oz sugar
2–3 drops vanilla essence
150 g/5 oz flour
a pinch of salt
100 g/3 ½ oz butter
grated rind of ½ untreated lemon
1 pinch cinnamon, cardamom and clove powder
3 tbsp custard powder
100 g/3 ½ oz grated cashew nuts
200 g/7 oz dried figs
butter for the tin
3 tbsp brandy
icing sugar (for dusting)
2 fresh figs to decorate
2 tbsp whole cashew nuts to decorate

Preparation time:
60 minutes
330 kcal/1385 kJ

1 Whisk eggs until creamy. Gradually mix in sugar, vanilla essence, flour and salt and whisk until the sugar has dissolved. Add the butter and mix well. Preheat the oven to 200 °C/390 °F/gas mark 6.

2 Stir in the grated lemon peel, spices, custard powder and grated cashew nuts. Rinse the dried figs, then dry and also stir into the mixture.

3 Grease a 24 cm/10 in spring-release tin, pour in the mixture and bake for about 35 minutes on the middle shelf of the oven.

4 Remove cake from the tin, sprinkle brandy onto it and allow to cool. Dust with icing sugar just before serving and decorate with slices of figs and cashew nuts.

Short Crust Pastry

Short Crust Pastry:

SHORT CRUST PASTRY

For a 26 cm/10 in spring-release tin

250 g/9 oz plain flour
125 g/4 ½ oz butter
1 egg
65 g/2 ½ oz sugar
a pinch of salt
fat to grease the tin
flour to dust the tin

Cake shown:
Tropical Tart
(below, recipe on page 43)

A short crust pastry is very quick and easy to make. The amount of fat and speedy mixing of the ingredients give this pastry its „short" character. Short crust pastry is ideal for thin flan bases, for mini flans and, when combined with other ingredients, is perfect for biscuits of all kinds. Short crust pastries can even be prepared in advance and will keep for about 8–10 days in the fridge in a sealed, air-tight container.

Sieve the flour onto the work surface and make a well at the centre.

Cut the butter into small pieces and arrange around the edge of the flour.

Crack the egg into a cup (to test for freshness).

Then put the egg into the well.

Basic Recipe

Sprinkle the sugar and flour round the edge of the flour.

For a fruit tart base, roll out the pastry thinly.

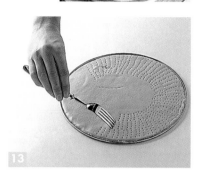

Prick the pastry several times to prevent air bubbles forming when baking.

Mix everything until the flour has been worked in completely.

Use the edge of the spring-release tin to cut out the base.

Put the spring-release tin over the base and lock in position.

Shape quickly and roll into a ball.

Wrap the cut-out pastry around a rolling pin.

Roll out the remaining pastry into a long roll or „sausage".

Wrap the ball in cling film and leave for about 30 minutes in a cool place.

Then unroll over the base of the spring-release tin.

Press the roll in position around the edge with your fingers.

35

SHORT CRUST PASTRY

Pineapple and Nut Cake

Makes 24 slices

300 g/10 ½ oz rye flour

200 g/7 oz butter (in small pieces)

170 g/6 oz icing sugar

a pinch of salt

grated rind of 1 untreated lemon

1 egg

700 g/1 lb 9 oz pineapple rings (tinned)

50 g/1 ¾ oz sugar

100 g/3 ½ oz cashew nuts

4 tbsp lemon juice

Preparation time:
50 minutes (plus cooling time)
189 kcal/795 kJ

1 Cut the butter into small pieces and mix with the flour, 70 g/2 ½ oz of the icing sugar, the salt, lemon peel and egg on the work surface. Make into a ball, wrap in cling film and leave for about 1 hour in a cool place. Preheat the oven to 200 °C/ 390 °F/gas mark 6.

2 Drain the pineapple rings and cut in half. Sprinkle with sugar and leave to soak. Chop the cashew nuts coarsely and put aside.

3 Spread the pastry onto a baking tray lined with baking parchment. Arrange the pineapple on top and sprinkle with the chopped cashew nuts. Bake for 20 minutes on the middle shelf of the oven.

4 Mix the remaining icing sugar with the lemon juice and brush over the cake when slightly cooled.

Apricot Cake with Meringue Topping

SHORT CRUST PASTRY

1 Make a short crust pastry mixture with the flour, butter, sugar, salt and egg. Wrap the pastry in cling film and leave for about 30 minutes in a cool place.

2 Preheat the oven to 200 °C/390 °F/gas mark 6. Peel the apricots and cut into slices.

3 Roll out the pastry and transfer to a baking tray lined with baking parchment. Brush pastry with the jam and arrange the apricots on top. Bake for about 30 minutes on the middle shelf of the oven.

4 Whisk egg whites until stiff, gradually add the icing sugar and almonds. Spread over the cake about 10 minutes before the end of baking time, then continue baking.

Makes 16 slices

250 g/9 oz plain flour
125 g/4 ½ oz butter
65 g/2 ½ oz sugar
a pinch of salt
1 egg
1 kg/2 lb 3 oz apricots
200 g/7 oz apricot jam
3 egg whites
100 g/3 ½ oz icing sugar
50 g/1 ¾ oz ground almonds

Preparation time:
60 minutes (plus cooling time)
169 kcal/713 kJ

SHORT CRUST PASTRY

Makes 24 slices

300 g/10 ½ oz plain flour

200 g/7 oz butter (in small pieces)

100 g/3 ½ oz sugar

a pinch of salt

grated rind of an untreated lemon

1 egg

1 Tsp ground all spice

500 g/1 lb 2 oz forest fruits (defrost if frozen)

3 tbsp lemon juice

1 tbsp rum

flour to dust the work surface

baking parchment

200 g white cooking chocolate

cashew nuts to decorate

icing sugar to dust

Preparation time:
30 minutes (plus cooling time)
171 kcal/721 kJ

Forest Fruits Cake

1 Add the small pieces of butter to the flour, sugar, salt, lemon peel, egg and ground all spice on the work surface and mix well. Then shape and roll into a ball, wrap in cling film and leave for about 1 hour in a cool place.

2 Preheat the oven to 200 °C/390 °F/gas mark 6. Sprinkle lemon juice and rum onto the forest fruits and leave for about 5 minutes to soak.

3 Roll out the pastry on the well-floured work surface, then transfer to a baking tray lined with baking parchment. Spread the forest fruits on top. Bake for 10 minutes on the middle shelf of the oven.

4 Melt the chocolate over hot water and use to decorate the cake. Decorate with cashew nuts and sprinkle with icing sugar.

Cheesecake

1 Preheat the oven to 200 °C/390 °F/gas mark 6. Make a short crust pastry with the flour, butter, egg and salt. Dust the work surface with flour, roll out the pastry and cut to size with the edge of a spring-release tin.

2 Spread the pastry over the base of a 26 cm/10 in greased spring-release tin and prick several times with a fork. Bake for about 18 minutes on the middle shelf of the oven. Remove from the tin and leave to cool on a cooling rack.

3 For the filling soak the gelatine in water. Clean and halve the strawberries. Mix the soft cheese, icing sugar and lemon juice until smooth.

4 Squeeze out the gelatine, dissolve in 4 tbsp water at a low temperature and add to the cheese mixture, stirring constantly. Whisk the cream until stiff and fold in well.

5 Put the spring-release tin over the baked pastry base, arrange half the strawberries on the base. Spread the cheese mixture on top and allow to set. Slice the remaining strawberries and arrange on top of the cheese mixture. Prepare the quick-jel and pour over the fruit. Slice lemon thinly and use to decorate the cake.

Makes 12 slices

250 g/9 oz plain flour
150 g/5 oz butter
1 egg
65 g/2 ½ oz sugar
a pinch of salt
8 leaves of gelatine
750 g/1 lb 11 oz strawberries
400 g/14 oz soft cheese
175 g/6 oz icing sugar
4 tbsp lemon juice
400 g/14 oz whipping cream
1 sachet red quick-jel
1 untreated lemon
flour to dust the work surface
butter for the tin

Preparation time:
1 hour 10 minutes
474 kcal/1991 kJ

Espresso Torte

Makes 12 slices

For the pastry:

2 tsp instant Espresso coffee powder

150 g/5 oz plain flour

1 tsp cocoa powder

40 g/1 ½ oz sugar

a pinch of salt

1 egg white

100 g/3 ½ oz butter

For the topping:

400 g/14 oz apricots (tinned)

6 sheets white leaf gelatine

500 g/1 lb 2 oz kefir or yoghurt

75 g/2 ½ oz sugar

2–3 drops vanilla essence

3 tbsp lemon juice

4 cl/1 fl oz almond liqueur

200 g/7 oz whipping cream

1 sachet clear quick-jel

whipped cream to decorate

cocoa powder for dusting

Preparation time:
45 minutes (plus cooling time)
270 kcal/1130 kJ

1 Mix the coffee powder with 1 tbsp hot water until smooth, then leave to cool. Make a smooth pastry with the flour, cocoa, sugar, salt, egg white, butter and coffee. Leave in a cool place for at least 30 minutes.

2 Preheat the oven to 200 °C/390 °F/ gas mark 6. Drain the apricots and leave 4 or 5 aside. Dice about ⅓ of the apricots and blend the rest.

3 Roll out the pastry and transfer to the base of a 26 cm/10 in spring-release tin. Bake for about 10 minutes on the middle shelf of the oven.

4 Leave the base to cool in the tin. Soak the gelatine in cold water. Mix the kefir or yoghurt with the sugar, vanilla essence, lemon juice and liqueur until smooth. Heat the blended apricot mixture. Dissolve the gelatine in this mixture. Add 3 tbsp kefir mixture.

5 Add the remaining kefir mixture and diced apricots, mix well and leave in a cool place. Whisk the cream until stiff. When the kefir mixture starts to set, stir in the cream. Spread the mixture evenly on top of the base. Leave for 4 hours in a cool place.

6 Halve the remaining apricots, cut into slices and use to decorate the cake. Make up the quick-jel mix as directed and pour over the apricots. Allow to set. Decorate with rosettes of whipped cream and dust with cocoa powder.

with Apricots

Fruit and Nut Tart

Makes 12 slices

300 g/10 ½ oz rye flour

200 g/7 oz butter
(in small pieces)

70 g/2 ½ oz icing sugar

a pinch of salt

grated rind of 1 untreated
lemon

1 egg

300 g/10 ½ oz mixed fruit
and nuts

200 g/7 oz soft cheese

1 pinch ground allspice

1 pinch aniseed powder

flour for the work surface

icing sugar to dust

redcurrants to decorate

Preparation time:
50 minutes (plus cooling time)
217 kcal/913 kJ

1 Mix the flour with the butter, icing sugar, salt, lemon peel and egg on a work surface, and roll into a ball. Wrap in cling film and leave for at least 1 hour in a cold place.

2 Preheat the oven to 200 °C/390 °F/gas mark 6. Mix the fruit and nuts with the soft cheese, allspice and aniseed.

3 Roll the pastry out on the well-floured work surface and line a 24 cm/10 in spring-release tin. Bake for about 15 minutes on the middle shelf of the oven.

4 Spread the cheese and fruit and nut mixture onto the base and bake for another 15 minutes. Dust with icing sugar and decorate with the redcurrants.

Tropical Tart

1 Add the flour to the flakes of butter, icing sugar, salt, lemon peel and egg on the work surface and mix well. Then shape and roll into a ball. Wrap in cling film and leave for about 1 hour to cool.

2 Preheat the oven to 200 °C/390 °F/ gas mark 6. Roll out the pastry on a well-floured work surface and line a 24 cm/ 10 in tart tin. Bake for about 15 minutes on the middle shelf of the oven.

3 Mix the raspberry liqueur with the soft cheese. Wash and dry the fruit, cut into slices or sticks. Sprinkle mixed lemon juice and vanilla essence on top.

4 Spread the soft cheese mixture over the tart base and decorate with the fruit.

Makes 12 slices

300 g/10 ½ oz plain flour

200 g/7 oz butter, in flakes

70 g/2 ½ oz icing sugar

a pinch of salt

½ tsp grated peel of 1 untreated lemon

1 egg

400 g/14 oz soft cheese

80 ml/2 ¾ fl oz raspberry liqueur

2 star fruits

1 small mango

3 kiwis

3 tbsp lemon juice

2–3 drops vanilla essence

flour for the work surface

Preparation time:
45 minutes (plus cooling time)
730 kcal/3066 kJ

Mandarin Cream Torte

1 Mix the flour with the almonds, baking powder, sugar, salt, vanilla essence, egg, egg yolk and butter to make a smooth short crust pastry. Leave for 1 hour in a cool place. Then cut chilled pastry into 4 portions. Preheat oven to 200 °C/390 °F/gas mark 6.

2 Roll each quarter out to fit a round 26 cm/10 in spring-release tin. Prick each several times with a fork. Bake each pastry base for about 15 minutes on the middle shelf of the oven.

3 Cut one of the bases into 8 slices while still warm. Allow all bases to cool. Pour the mandarins into a sieve and drain well. Keep the juice.

4 Soak the gelatine in cold water. Whisk the cream until stiff, gradually adding the sugar.

5 Heat 200 ml/7 fl oz of the mandarin juice. Squeeze out the gelatine and dissolve in the juice. Allow to cool. As soon as the mixture starts to set, stir into the cream.

6 Pour ¾ of the cream into an icing bag with hole nozzle and pipe in circles over the short crust bases. Arrange the mandarins on the bases. Place the bases carefully one on top of another. Arrange the 8 slices on top of the torte and decorate with the remaining cream.

Makes 8 slices

For the pastry:
300 g/10 ½ oz plain flour
175 g/6 oz ground almonds
1 tsp baking powder
125 g/4 ½ oz sugar
a pinch of salt
5–6 drops vanilla essence
1 egg
1 egg yolk
200 g/7 oz butter

For the filling:
2 tins mandarins (175 g/6 oz drained weight per tin)
6 sheets white leaf gelatine
600 g/1 lb 5 oz whipping cream
75 g/2 ½ oz sugar
50 g/1 ¾ oz flaked almonds

Preparation time:
1 hour 30 minutes
(plus cooling time)
569 kcal/2391 kJ

Semolina Cheesecake

Makes 12 slices

For the pastry:
80 g/2 ¾ oz sugar
150 g/5 oz butter
300 g/10 ½ oz plain flour
1 egg
a pinch of salt
butter to grease the tin

For the filling:
4 eggs
1 egg white
750 g/1 lb 11 oz low-fat quark or soft cheese
180 g/6 ½ oz sugar
grated zest of an untreated lemon
4 tbsp lemon juice
80 g/2 ¾ oz butter
50 g/1 ¾ oz custard powder
1 tbsp baking powder
75 g/2 ½ oz soft wheat semolina
450 g/1 lb raspberries (defrosted if frozen)
icing sugar to dust

Preparation time:
50 minutes (plus resting time)
230 kcal/970 kJ

1 Mix the sugar, butter, flour, 1 egg and pinch of salt into a smooth pastry, and allow to rest for about 30 minutes. Preheat the oven to 175 °C/345 °F/gas mark 3 ½.

2 Roll out the pastry onto a greased baking tray. Bake for 15 minutes in the oven, then allow to cool. Increase the temperature of the oven to 200 °C/390 °F/gas mark 6.

3 Separate the eggs. Mix the quark or soft cheese, sugar, egg yolks, lemon zest and lemon juice. Melt the butter, allow to cool, then add to the quark mixture. Mix the custard powder, baking powder and semolina and stir into the quark mixture.

4 Whisk the egg whites until stiff, stir the raspberries in carefully. Spread over the pastry base and bake for about 30 minutes at 200 °C/390 °F/gas mark 6. Allow to cool and cut into slices. Sprinkle with icing sugar (optional).

Covered Apricot Cake

1 Mix the flour with the butter, milk, sugar, egg yolks and salt to make a smooth pastry, roll into a ball, wrap in cling film and leave for about 1 hour in a cool place.

2 Wash the apricots, dry, cut in half and stone. Wash the star fruit, dry and cut into slices. Grease a 24 cm/10 in spring-release tin with butter, and coat with the crumbled sponge biscuits. Preheat the oven to 225 °C/440 °F/gas mark 7.

3 Roll out the pastry onto a floured work surface and line the tin. Place the fruits on top, cut off the overlapping pastry and press the edge in position.

4 Roll out the remaining pastry into a round shape and cover the cake with it. Brush the pastry with the beaten egg and prick several times with a fork. Bake for about 25 minutes on the middle shelf of the oven.

5 Sprinkle with icing sugar before serving.

Makes 12 slices

250 g/9 oz plain flour
130 g/4 ½ oz butter
1 tbsp milk
100 g/3 ½ oz sugar
2 egg yolks
a pinch of salt
100 g/3 ½ oz finely crumbled sponge biscuits
600 g/1 lb 5 oz apricots
1 star fruit
1 egg for the glaze
icing sugar to dust
flour for the work surface
butter for the tin

Preparation time:
50 minutes (plus cooling time)
250 kcal/1050 kJ

Yeast Dough

Yeast Dough:

For 1 tray

¼ l/9 fl oz milk

40 g/1 ½ oz fresh yeast

500 g/1 lb 2 oz plain flour

60 g/2 oz sugar

a pinch of salt

1 egg

100 g/3 ½ oz softened butter

butter for the tray

flour for the work surface

For a sugar cake:

add

100 g/3 ½ oz butter

100 g/3 ½ oz sugar

½ tsp ground cinnamon

Cake shown
Thuringian Crumble Cake
(below, recipe page 58/59)

Yeast dough is the basis of many delicious sweet and savoury cakes. Making up a yeast dough is not as complicated as you might think, but it does take a bit longer than the preparation of other pastries. The main reason is that the yeast bacteria need time to work so that your cake rises properly. They work best at a room temperature of about 25–30 °C/77–86 °F.

Crumble fresh yeast into tepid milk and allow to dissolve.

Stir in a little flour until the mixture thickens. Add 1 tsp sugar.

Cover the mixture and leave for about 30 minutes to rise.

Sieve the remaining flour into a bowl.

Basic Recipe

5 With your hand, make a well at the centre.

9 Add the yeast mixture.

13 Allow the dough to stand until it has doubled its size, then knead again.

6 Arrange the remaining sugar and salt around the edge of the well.

10 Knead everything well by hand.

14 Place the dough on the well-greased baking tray and roll out till even and smooth.

7 Break the egg into a cup, then put into the well.

11 Knead dough vigorously until it forms air bubbles.

15 Brush with melted butter for a butter cake.

8 Cut the butter into small pieces and arrange around the edge of the well.

12 Roll dough into a ball, cover with a tea towel or foil.

16 Sprinkle with sugar and cinnamon. Allow to rise for another 10–20 minutes before baking.

Crunchy Nut Cake

Makes 24 slices

160 ml/5 fl oz (= ¼ pint) milk

400 g/14 oz plain flour

30 g/1 oz fresh yeast

160 g/5 ½ oz butter

40 g/1 ½ oz sugar

a pinch of salt

1 egg

1 egg yolk

250 g/9 oz pecan nuts

250 g/9 oz raisins

250 g/9 oz brown sugar

250 g/9 oz whipping cream

250 g/9 oz coarsely chopped peanuts

6 tbsp whisky

Preparation time:
1 hour 15 minutes (plus resting time)
320 kcal/1345 kJ

1 Heat the milk in a pan. Sieve the flour into a bowl, make a well at the centre and crumble the yeast into the well. Pour in the milk. Knead and leave to stand for about 20 minutes in a warm place.

2 Knead 60 g/2 oz butter, sugar, salt, egg and egg yolk into the dough. Roll into a ball, cover and leave to rise until the dough has doubled in size. Preheat the oven to 200 °C/390 °F/gas mark 6.

3 Chop the pecan nuts and raisins coarsely. Melt the remaining butter in a pan with the brown sugar, stir in the cream and simmer for a short time. Stir in the chopped peanuts, the nut and raisin mixture and the whisky.

4 Roll out the dough onto a baking tray lined with baking parchment. Spread the nut mixture on top of the dough and bake for about 30 minutes on the middle shelf of the oven. Cut into triangles when cool.

Apple Cake

1 Grate the zest of both lemons, squeeze out the juice.

2 Mix the flour with the yeast. Add the milk, half of the lemon zest and the lemon juice, 80 g/2 ¾ oz sugar, 160 g/5 ½ oz butter and the egg. Knead into a smooth dough, cover and allow to stand until doubled in size.

3 Knead the dough once more, then roll out on a greased baking tray and allow to stand for another 15 minutes. Preheat the oven to 200 °C/390 °F/gas mark 6.

4 For the filling, whisk the remaining butter and sugar until smooth and creamy. Stir in the quark, the cream, the remaining zest and the custard powder.

5 Spread the mixture onto the dough. Peel the apples, quarter, remove the core and cut into slices. Arrange on top of the quark mixture.

6 Sprinkle with almond sticks and raisins, then bake for 40 minutes on the second shelf from the bottom. Pass the apricot jam through a sieve and spread over the cooled cake.

Makes 20 slices

2 untreated lemons
500 g/1 lb 2 oz plain flour
1 sachet dried yeast
¼ l/9 fl oz tepid milk
230 g/8 oz sugar
220 g/8 oz softened butter
1 egg
500 g/1 lb 2 oz low-fat quark or soft cheese
200 g cream
50 g/1 ¾ oz custard powder
1.5 kg/3 lb 5 oz apples
40 g/1 ½ oz almond sticks
40 g/1 ½ oz raisins
100 g/3 ½ oz apricot jam
butter to grease the tray

Preparation time:
60 minutes (plus resting time)
317 kcal/1332 kJ

53

Cheesecake Slices

Makes 18 slices

250 g/9 oz plain flour
1/2 sachet dried yeast
100 ml/3 ½ fl oz milk
grated zest of ½ untreated lemon
1 tbsp sugar
400 g/14 oz quark or soft cheese
2 eggs
2–3 drops vanilla essence
1 tsp grated lemon zest
20 g/¾ oz almond sticks
40 g/1 ½ oz flaked hazelnuts

Preparation time:
50 minutes (plus resting time)
101 kcal/428 kJ

1 Sieve the flour into a bowl and make a well at the centre. Dissolve the yeast in 1 tbsp tepid water, pour into the well, dust with a little flour from round the edge, and allow to rest for about 20 minutes.

2 Work in the milk, lemon zest and sugar and knead to a smooth dough. Allow to rest for another 20 minutes. Knead once more. Roll the dough out to make a thin base, and place on a baking tray lined with baking parchment. Cover and allow to rest again. Preheat the oven to 175 °C/345 °F/ gas mark 3 ½.

3 Mix the quark with the egg yolk, sugar and lemon zest until creamy and smooth. Whisk the egg white until stiff, then carefully fold into the quark mixture. Spread the mixture evenly onto the dough base.

4 Sprinkle with almond and hazel sticks. Bake for 20 minutes at 175 °C/345 °F/ gas mark 3 ½ on the middle shelf of the oven, then increase the temperature to 200 °C/ 390 °F/gas mark 6 and bake for another 15 minutes. Remove from the oven, allow to cool slightly, and serve warm.

with Hazelnuts

Cape Gooseberry Cake

Makes 24 slices

160 ml/5 fl oz (= ¼ pint) milk

400 g/14 oz strong white flour

30 g/1 oz fresh yeast

260 g/9 oz butter

40 g/1 ½ oz sugar

a pinch of salt

1 egg

2 egg yolks

100 g/3 ½ oz honey

150 g/5 oz plain flour

500 g/1 lb 2 oz cape gooseberries

flour for the work surface

100 g/3 ½ oz walnuts

Preparation time:
60 minutes (plus resting time)
200 kcal/842 kJ

1 Heat the milk in a pan. Sieve the flour into a bowl, make a well in the centre, and crumble the yeast into the well. Pour the milk in, knead and leave for about 20 minutes in a warm place to rise.

2 Knead in 60 g/2 oz butter, sugar, salt, egg and egg yolk. Roll into a ball, cover and allow to stand until double in size. Preheat the oven to 200 °C/390 °F/gas mark 6.

3 Whisk the remaining butter with the honey until smooth and creamy. Add the remaining egg yolk and flour and make a crumble mixture. Wash and halve the Cape gooseberries.

4 Roll the dough out on a well-floured work surface and place on a baking tray lined with baking parchment. Arrange the gooseberries on the dough, and cover with the crumble mixture. Sprinkle with walnuts. Bake for 40 minutes on the middle shelf of the oven.

Pear and Vanilla Cake

1 Heat 160 ml/5 fl oz (= ¼ pint) milk in a pan. Sieve the flour into a bowl, make a well in the centre and crumble the yeast into the well. Pour the milk in, knead, and leave for about 20 minutes in a warm place to rise.

2 Knead in 60 g/2 oz butter, 40 g sugar, salt, 1 egg and egg yolk. Roll the dough into a ball, cover and leave to stand until it has doubled in size. Preheat the oven to 200 °C/390 °F/gas mark 6.

3 Drain the pears and cut into slices. Mix the remaining milk with the custard powder and 2 tbsp sugar. Stir in the remaining butter.

4 Separate the eggs. Stir in the quark, pear brandy, pears, pulp of the vanilla pod and the egg yolk. Whisk the egg white until stiff and fold in.

5 Roll out the dough and place on a baking tray lined with baking parchment. Pour the pear mixture on top and bake for about 20 minutes on the middle shelf of the oven. When ready sprinkle with icing sugar.

Makes 24 slices

460 ml/16 fl oz milk
400 g/14 oz plain flour
30 g/1 oz fresh yeast
210 g/7 ½ oz butter
80 g/2 ¾ oz sugar
a pinch of salt
5 eggs
1 egg yolk
300 g/10 ½ oz pears (tinned)
50 g/1 ¾ oz custard powder
300 g/10 ½ oz cream quark or soft cheese
2 cl/1/2 fl oz pear brandy
pulp of 1 vanilla pod
icing sugar to dust

Preparation time:
60 minutes (plus resting time)
202 kcal/848 kJ

Crumble Cake

1 Sieve the flour and dried yeast into a mixing bowl and carefully mix. Add sugar, vanilla essence, salt, egg, milk and 50 g/1 ¾ oz of the melted butter. Knead to a smooth dough.

2 Cover and leave to stand for about 15 minutes. Dust dough lightly with flour, then remove from the bowl and knead briefly on the work surface. Roll out onto a greased baking tray (38 x 38 cm, or 15 x 15 in). Preheat the oven to 200 °C/390 °F/gas mark 6.

3 Brush the dough with the remaining butter. Fold a strip of aluminium foil and place around the outside of the dough so that it does not run over the edges of the tray.

4 For the crumble sieve the wheat flour into a mixing bowl. Mix with sugar and vanilla essence and add the softened butter. Using the dough hook on the electric mixer, work everything to make crumble of the required size.

5 Sprinkle half the crumble generously onto the dough. Fold cocoa powder into the remaining crumble. Fill in the spaces to form a black-and-white pattern.

6 Leave the dough and crumble mixture in a warm place to rise. After about 10 minutes put it into the oven and bake for 18 minutes on the middle shelf.

7 Meanwhile heat the milk and melt the butter in it. Sprinkle over the cake. When the cake is cold brush with melted butter and dust with icing sugar.

Makes 20 slices

375 g/13 oz plain flour
1 sachet dried yeast
50 g/1 ¾ oz sugar
2–3 drops vanilla essence
a pinch of salt
1 egg
200 ml/7 fl oz tepid milk
70 g/2 ½ oz melted, cooled butter
300 g/10 ½ oz plain wheat flour
150 g/5 oz sugar
2–3 drops vanilla essence
200 g/7 oz softened butter
10 g/⅓ oz cocoa powder
125 ml/4 ½ fl oz milk
60 g/2 oz butter
100 g/3 ½ oz melted butter
50 g/1 ¾ oz icing sugar
flour for the work surface

Preparation time:
60 minutes (plus resting time)
303 kcal/1273 kJ

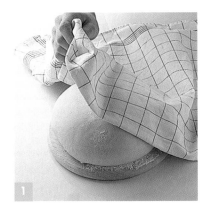

Plum Cake

Makes 16 slices

½ l/18 fl oz milk
40 g/1 ½ oz fresh yeast
500 g/1 lb 2 oz plain flour
80 g/2 ¾ oz sugar
a pinch of salt
1 egg
100 g/3 ½ oz butter
25 g/1 oz custard powder
1 egg yolk
200 g/7 oz marzipan
1.5 kg/3 lb 5 oz fresh plums
2 tbsp apricot jam
2 tbsp icing sugar
icing sugar to dust
flour for the work surface
butter for the tray

Preparation time:
1 hour 15 minutes (plus resting time)
385 kcal/1620 kJ

1 Make up a yeast dough with ¼ l/9 fl oz tepid milk, yeast, flour, sugar, salt, egg and butter. Allow the dough to rest until it has doubled in size.

2 Make vanilla cream with the milk, egg yolk, sugar and custard powder. Crumble the marzipan into small pieces and stir into the vanilla cream, sprinkle with icing sugar and allow to cool.

3 Once the dough has risen, divide in half and roll each piece out on a well-floured work surface to cover a baking tray. Place one of the dough bases on a greased baking tray. Preheat the oven to 200 °C/390 °F/gas mark 6.

4 Spread the cooled marzipan and vanilla cream on top of the dough base. Wash the plums, halve, and stone. Arrange on top of the marzipan cream, with the open side uppermost.

5 Carefully place the second dough base on top and press gently in place. Prick the surface several times with a fork, then allow the cake to rise for about another 20 minutes.

6 Bake on the middle shelf of the oven for about 45 minutes. Strain the apricot jam through a sieve and brush it on the still warm cake. When the jam has set, dust the cake with icing sugar.

Cherry Slices

250 g/9 oz plain flour

½ packet dried yeast

130 ml/4 ½ fl oz tepid milk

60 g/2 oz sugar

a pinch of salt

40 g/1 ½ oz butter

2 eggs

1 tsp grated zest of an untreated lemon

1 jar Morello cherries (460 g/1 lb drained weight)

100 g/3 ½ oz crème fraîche

25 g/1 oz custard powder

2–3 drops vanilla essence

butter for the tray

flour for the work surface

icing sugar to dust

Preparation time:
40 minutes (plus resting time)
275 kcal/1157 kJ

1 Mix the flour and yeast in a bowl. Add 100 ml/3 ½ fl oz milk, 50 g/1 ¾ oz sugar, salt, butter, 1 egg and the lemon zest and knead everything to make a smooth dough. Cover and leave to rest until it has doubled in size.

2 Pour the cherries into a sieve and drain. Separate the remaining egg. Stir the egg yolk into the crème fraîche, custard powder, vanilla essence and sugar. Whisk the egg white until stiff and fold in. Preheat the oven to 200 °C/390 °F/gas mark 6.

3 Knead the dough again briefly on the well-floured work surface and roll out to a rectangle measuring 25 x 35 cm (about 10 x 14 in). Place the dough onto a greased baking tray. Roll over the edges to make a rim about 2 cm (¾ in) wide and press in position with a fork. Spread the cream mixture onto the dough, and add the cherries.

4 Brush the edges of the dough with the milk and bake on the middle shelf of the preheated oven for 25 minutes. Allow to cool, then dust with icing sugar.

61

Sponges

Sponges :

For one 24–26 cm
(9–10 in) spring-
release baking tin

4 eggs
2 tbsp tepid water
120 g/4 ¼ oz sugar
75 g/2 ½ oz plain flour
75 g/2 ½ oz cornflour
a pinch of salt
baking parchment for
the tin

Cake shown
Sponge Torte
(below, recipe page 70)

A sponge is a most exquisite mix of eggs, sugar and flour. The high proportion of egg – a combination of beaten yolk cream and stiff egg white – makes this a particularly fine and light cake mixture. There is even a recipe dating from 1805 in which it is recommended to „beat the yolk of 13 eggs until smooth and creamy". Nowadays, even the finest sponge is made with fewer eggs. A food processor or hand mixer can be used to make this type of cake very light. Follow each step of the recipe carefully and your sponge will be a masterpiece.

Separate the eggs. Ensure that the bowl used for the egg white is absolutely clean and fat-free.

Add the tepid water to the egg yolks. Use the mixer to beat until creamy.

Gradually add ⅔ of the sugar.

Continue whisking until the mixture is thick and creamy.

Basic Recipe

5 Whisk the egg white until stiff. Gradually add the remaining sugar and salt.

9 Carefully fold egg white and flour mixture into the cream until smooth and creamy.

13 Carefully ease the cake mixture away from the sides of the tin with a sharp knife.

6 Carefully fold ⅓ of the stiff egg white mixture into the egg yolk cream. Pour the remaining egg white on top.

10 Line the base of a spring-release tin with baking parchment.

14 Open the spring-release tin and carefully lift away from the cake.

7 Mix the plain flour with the cornflour.

11 Pour the sponge mixture into the tin. Level the surface with a spatula.

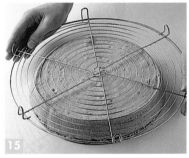

15 Place a cooling rack on top of the still warm sponge.

8 Sieve the mixture onto the egg white.

12 When baked, leave the sponge in the baking tin and allow to cool on a cooling rack.

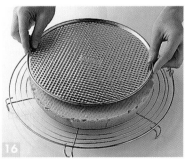

16 Turn the cake over and remove the baking parchment.

Apricot Slices

Makes 12 slices

8 eggs

200 g/7 oz sugar

a pinch of salt

100 g/3 ½ oz plain flour

100 g/3 ½ oz ground hazelnuts

¼ tsp baking powder

¼ tsp cinnamon

6 sheets white leaf gelatine

juice and zest of 2 untreated lemons

¼ l/9 fl oz dry white wine

4 cl Armagnac

125 g/4 ½ oz whipping cream

500 g/1 lb 2 oz apricots

icing sugar to dust

Preparation time:
50 minutes
281 kcal/1181 kJ

1 Preheat the oven to 200 °C/390 °F/ gas mark 6. Separate the eggs. Make up a sponge mixture with 5 egg yolks, 4 tbsp water, 150 g sugar, 4 egg whites, salt, flour, hazelnuts, baking powder and cinnamon. Pour the mixture onto a baking tray lined with baking parchment and smooth out with a spatula.

2 Bake for about 15 minutes on the middle shelf of the oven. Then turn out onto a cooling rack and remove the parchment. Allow the sponge to cool and cut evenly into slices each 10 cm wide.

3 Soak the gelatine in the water. Whisk the remaining egg yolk with the remaining sugar, lemon juice, lemon zest, white wine and Armagnac in a bowl until creamy.

4 Stand in hot water, then whisk until thick. Squeeze out the gelatine and dissolve at a moderate temperature, stir in the egg cream gradually.

5 Separately whisk the egg white and whipping cream until stiff, then carefully fold into the cooled cream mixture just before this sets. Leave a little cream aside, spread the rest on half of the sponge slices.

6 Wash and dry the apricots, cut into slices and arrange on top of the cream, leaving a few aside. Place the remaining sponge slices on top, decorate with the cream and apricots, then dust with icing sugar.

Charlotte

1 Preheat the oven to 225 °C/440 °F/ gas mark 7. Whisk the eggs until foamy. Add 4 tbsp water and continue whisking until light and airy. Add sugar, salt and vanilla essence. Whisk until the sugar has dissolved and it becomes creamy.

2 Mix the flour, cornflour and baking powder, sieve into the egg mixture and fold in. Spread the mixture onto a baking tray lined with baking parchment and bake for about 12 minutes. Then loosen the edge with a sharp knife and turn onto a kitchen towel sprinkled with sugar. Remove the parchment.

3 Spread the jam over the sponge mix and roll up. Finally allow to cool and cut into slices. Soak the gelatine in the water. Separate the eggs.

4 Whisk the egg white and 4 tbsp water until foamy. Drizzle in the sugar, then add ¼ of the orange and lemon juice. Dissolve the gelatine in the remaining juice and add to the mixture. Leave in a cool place.

5 Whisk the egg whites until stiff and fold into the egg yolk mixture. Line a bowl with the sponge slices and pour in the orange cream. Leave in the fridge to set. Turn out just before serving.

Makes 8 slices

For the sponge:
4 eggs
200 g/7 oz sugar
a pinch of salt
2–3 drops vanilla essence
80 g/2 ¾ oz plain flour
80 g/2 ¾ oz cornflour
1 tsp baking powder
sugar for dusting

For the filling:
400 g/14 oz raspberry jam
9 sheets white leaf gelatine
3 eggs
100 g/3 ½ oz sugar
juice of 5 oranges
juice of 1 lemon

Preparation time:
50 minutes (plus chilling time)
318 kcal/1336 kJ

Port Wine Slices

Makes 12 slices

For the sponge:

4 eggs
120 g/4 ¼ oz sugar
a pinch of salt
75 g/2 ½ oz plain flour
75 g/2 ½ oz cornflour

For the filling:

9 sheets white leaf gelatine
1 jar Morello cherries (460 g/1 lb drained weight)
250 g/9 oz creamy yoghurt
100 g/3 ½ oz sugar
2 tbsp port wine
200 g/7 oz whipping cream

For the topping:

200 g/7 oz whipping cream
2–3 drops vanilla essence
cocoa powder
sugar for dusting

Preparation time:
45 minutes (plus chilling time)
298 kcal/1254 kJ

1 Preheat the oven to 200 °C/390 °F/ gas mark 6. Make a sponge mixture with the eggs, 2 tbsp tepid water, sugar, salt, flour and cornflour. Spread the sponge mixture on a baking tray lined with baking parchment.

2 Bake for about 12 minutes on the middle shelf of the oven. Turn onto a kitchen towel sprinkled with sugar. Allow to cool.

3 For the cream soak the gelatine in cold water. Drain the cherries and blend in a mixer. Mix the pureed cherries with the yoghurt, sugar and port wine. Squeeze out the gelatine and dissolve in a little water at a moderate temperature, then stir into the cherry-yoghurt mixture. Whisk the cream until stiff. When the cherry-yoghurt mixture starts to set, carefully fold in the whipped cream. Remove the parchment from the sponge base.

4 Cut horizontally through the middle of the sponge base. Cut aluminium foil into strips about 1 m x 5 cm (39 x 2 in), wrap firmly around one half of the sponge base and hold in position with paper clips.

5 Spread the cherry cream evenly over the sponge base, then cover with the 2nd sponge base. Press down slightly and leave in the fridge until set. Whisk the whipping cream and vanilla essence together until stiff, then spread over the sponge. Remove the aluminium foil.

6 With a pastry comb or fork make wavy lines on the top layer. Cut into 12 slices. Sprinkle with cocoa powder to decorate.

Chocolate Sponge

1 Preheat the oven to 180 °C/355 °F/ gas mark 4. Separate the eggs and whisk the egg whites until stiff. Drizzle in the sugar and continue to whisk until the sugar has dissolved.

2 Mix the flour with the baking powder, then stir into the egg white along with the chocolate, pumpkin seeds and egg yolks. Finally add the melted butter and the rum. Stir until the mixture is smooth.

3 Pour the sponge mixture into a greased loaf tin and bake for about 45 minutes. With a wooden cocktail stick or knitting needle check to see if the cake is done. If the stick comes out clean, the cake is ready.

Makes 10 slices

5 eggs
100 g/3 ½ oz sugar
500 g/1 lb 2 oz plain flour
1 tsp baking powder
100 g/3 ½ oz grated chocolate
3 tsp grated pumpkin seeds
30 g/1 oz melted butter
2 tbsp rum
butter to grease the tin

Preparation time:
60 minutes
324 kcal/1355 kJ

69

Sponge Torte

Makes 12 slices

4 eggs

150 g/5 oz sugar

2–3 drops vanilla essence

160 g plain flour

3 tsp baking powder

50 g grated hazelnuts

150 g lime marmalade

zest and juice of 2–3 untreated limes

750 g/1 lb 11 oz yoghurt

100 g/3 ½ oz sugar

3 tbsp white wine

3 egg whites

200 g/7 oz whipping cream

9 sheets leaf gelatine

500 g/1 lb 2 oz whipping cream

2 limes to decorate

Preparation time:
1 hour 30 minutes
(plus chilling time)
434 kcal/1817 kJ

1 Preheat the oven to 180 °C/355 °F/ gas mark 4. Separate the eggs. Beat the egg yolk with the sugar and vanilla essence. Whisk the egg white until stiff. Sieve the flour and baking powder into the egg yolk mixture. Add the egg white and the hazelnuts. Pour the mixture into a greased 26 cm/10 in spring-release baking tin, level the top and bake for 40 minutes. Allow to cool.

2 Cut the sponge through horizontally twice and spread with marmalade. Grate the limes, squeeze out the juice and mix both with the yoghurt, sugar and wine. Separately whisk egg white and 200 g/7 oz whipping cream until stiff. Dissolve the gelatine and stir into the cream and egg white.

3 Place the ring on top of one cake base. Spread with ⅓ of the cream, place the second base on top and spread with another ⅓ of the cream. Place the last base on top and spread this with the remaining cream. Leave in the fridge for two hours to chill.

4 Whisk the remaining whipping cream until stiff. Cut the limes into thin slices and decorate the torte with whipped cream around the edge and lime slices.

Quick Strawberry Torte

1 Preheat the oven to 200 °C/390 °F/ gas mark 6. Make up a sponge mixture with the eggs, water, 120 g/4 ¼ oz sugar, salt, flour and cornflour. Pour the mixture into a 26 cm/10 in spring-release baking tin lined with baking parchment and bake for 30 minutes on the second shelf from the bottom of the oven.

2 Wash the strawberries and remove the stalks. Leave 12 strawberries aside. Halve the rest. Whisk the cream and sugar until stiff.

3 Cut the cooled sponge base through twice horizontally. Cover two of the bases with half of the strawberries each and ⅓ of the cream. Then place one on top of the other.

4 Place the third base on top. Cover the torte with the remaining cream (again, leave some aside). Decorate with 12 rosettes of whipped cream and strawberries. Sprinkle flaked almonds around the sides.

Makes 12 slices

4 eggs
2 tbsp tepid water
150 g/5 oz sugar
a pinch of salt
75 g/2 ½ oz plain flour
75 g/2 ½ oz cornflour
750 g/1 lb 11 oz strawberries
750 g/1 lb 11 oz whipping cream
50 g/1 ¾ oz flaked roast almonds

Preparation time:
45 minutes
336 kcal/1413 kJ

Peach Sponge

Makes 12 slices

4 eggs
2 tbsp tepid water
120 g/4 ¼ oz sugar
75 g/2 ½ oz plain flour
75 g/2 1/2 oz ground
almonds
a pinch of salt
¼ tsp ground cloves
½ tsp ground cinnamon
3 peaches
3 tbsp peach liqueur
icing sugar for dusting

Preparation time:
1 hour 15 minutes
153 kcal/645 kJ

1 Separate the eggs. Beat the egg yolks, water and half of the sugar to make a creamy mixture. Whisk the egg whites with the remaining sugar until stiff.

2 Mix the flour with the almonds and spices. Stir ⅓ of the egg white into the egg yolk mixture, then fold in the remaining egg white and flour mixture.

3 Pour the mixture onto the base of a 24 cm/10 in spring-release baking tin lined with baking parchment. Preheat the oven to 180 °C/355 °F/gas mark 4.

4 Peel the peaches, remove the stones and cut into thin slices. Arrange the slices over the cake mixture and bake for about 50 minutes on the middle shelf of the oven.

5 Prick the surface of the cake several times with a fork, sprinkle with liqueur and allow to cool in the tin on a cooling rack. Then turn the cake onto a cooling rack and remove the parchment. Sprinkle the sponge with icing sugar before serving.

Caramel Cheesecake

1 Preheat the oven to 150 °C/300 °F/ gas mark 2. Grease a 24 cm/10 in spring-release baking tin. Crumble the sponge biscuits and spread over the base of the baking tin.

2 Whisk the cream cheese with a mixer until smooth. Add the sugar, egg white, vanilla extract and continue whisking for 2 minutes on a medium setting. Add the flour and yoghurt, and mix until smooth.

3 Spread the cream mixture over the crumbled sponge biscuits. Bake for 60 minutes in the oven, then switch off and leave to rest in the oven for another 30 minutes with the door shut. Remove from the oven and allow to cool for 15 minutes, then cover and leave for at least three hours in the fridge to set.

4 Remove the spring-release tin. Spoon the caramel sauce over the cake and decorate with walnut halves. Keep the cake cool until serving.

Makes 12 slices

15 sponge biscuits
400 g/14 oz cream cheese
150 g/5 oz sugar
3 egg whites
2 tsp vanilla extract
2 tbsp plain flour
400 g/14 oz vanilla yoghurt
80 ml caramel sauce (ready-made)
walnut halves to decorate
butter to grease the tin

Preparation time:
1 hour 50 minutes
(plus chilling time)
175 kcal/732 kJ

Red Wine Slices

Makes 12 slices

For the sponge:

1 egg
2 egg yolks
2 tbsp hot water
2 tsp sugar
2 egg whites
50 g/1 ¾ oz plain flour
25 g/1 oz cornflour
1 tsp baking powder

For the topping:

ground arrowroot or white gelatine
2 egg yolks
150 ml/5 fl oz (= ¼ pint) dry red wine
100 ml/3 ½ fl oz grape juice
2 egg whites
100 g/3 ½ oz grapes

Preparation time:
50 minutes
82 kcal/369 kJ

1 Whisk the egg, egg yolk, water and 1 tsp sugar until foamy. Whisk the egg white until stiff and add to the egg yolk mixture. Sieve the flour, cornflour and baking powder on top of this mixture. Fold in lightly. Preheat the oven to 200 °C/ 390 °F/gas mark 6.

2 Line just half of a baking tray with baking parchment. Turn parchment up along the outside. Pour in the sponge mixture and level off with a spatula. Bake for about 12 minutes on the middle shelf of the oven.

3 Turn onto a kitchen towel and remove the parchment. Allow to cool. Allow the gelatine to soak for 10 minutes in 5 tbsp cold water. Whisk the egg yolk with the remaining sugar until creamy.

4 Add the red wine and the grape juice. Heat the gelatine until it is dissolved, then stir into the red wine mixture. Whisk the egg white until very stiff, and fold into the red wine mixture as this sets. Spread the cream over the sponge base. Allow to cool.

5 Wash the grapes, halve and arrange on the set cream. Cut into twelve slices before serving.

Nut Sponge

Makes 12 slices

70 g/2 ½ oz pine nuts

70 g/2 ½ oz unpeeled almonds

70 g/2 ½ oz walnuts

100 g/3 ½ oz plain chocolate

4 egg whites

175 g/6 oz sugar

4 egg yolks

30 g breadcrumbs

pulp of 1 vanilla pod

1 tsp baking powder

2 tbsp rum

2 tbsp milk

butter and breadcrumbs for the baking tin

icing sugar for dusting

Preparation time:
1 hour 20 minutes
262 kcal/1097 kJ

1 Finely grind pine nuts, almonds and walnuts. Grate the chocolate finely. Whisk the egg white until stiff, drizzle in 75 g/ 2 ½ oz sugar and whisk until the sugar is dissolved. Preheat the oven to 175 °C/345 °F/ gas mark 3 ½.

2 Beat the egg yolks with 100 g/3 ½ oz sugar until creamy. Mix the ground nuts and chocolate with the breadcrumbs, the vanilla pulp and the baking powder and fold into the egg yolk mixture alternately with the rum and milk. Carefully fold in the egg white.

3 Grease a 25 cm/10 in loaf tin and dust with breadcrumbs. Pour in the sponge mix and bake for 60 minutes in the lower half of the oven.

4 Allow the cake to cool in the tin, then turn out and dust with icing sugar. Serve with whipped cream and chopped walnuts.

Swiss Roll

1 Preheat the oven to 200 °C/390 °F/gas mark 6. For the sponge separate the eggs, then beat the egg yolks to a creamy consistency with the sugar, vanilla essence and salt. Whisk the egg whites until stiff.

2 Mix the flour with the cornflour and baking powder and fold into the egg cream together with the egg white. Line a large baking tray with baking parchment.

3 Pour the sponge mixture evenly over the baking tray and bake for 12 minutes on the middle shelf of the oven. Lay out a clean tea towel on the work surface and sprinkle with a little sugar.

4 Remove the sponge from the oven and carefully turn immediately onto the towel. Remove the baking parchment. Leave aside until it is filled. Remove the stalks from the strawberries and wash. Cut half of them up very small and cook for 2 minutes with the jam.

5 Mix the Mascarpone with the icing sugar, vanilla essence, almond liqueur, 2 tbsp milk and 2 tbsp cream, then heat in a pan. Whisk the remaining cream until stiff. Fold ⅔ of this into the Mascarpone cream. Soak the gelatine, dissolve and fold into the Mascarpone cream.

6 Spread the Mascarpone cream and strawberries onto the sponge base and roll up. Leave for about 2 hours in the fridge. Decorate with the remaining cream and strawberries, and dust with a little cocoa powder.

Makes 12 slices

For the sponge:
4 eggs
125 g/4 ½ oz sugar
2–3 drops vanilla essence
a pinch of salt
75 g/2 ½ oz plain flour
75 g/2 ½ oz cornflour
1 tsp baking powder
sugar for dusting

For the filling:
250 g/9 oz strawberries
225 g/8 oz strawberry jam
250 g/9 oz Mascarpone
50 g/1 ¾ oz icing sugar
2–3 drops vanilla essence
2 tbsp almond liqueur
4 tbsp milk
200 g/7 oz whipping cream
2 sheets leaf gelatine
cocoa powder for dusting

Preparation time:
50 minutes (plus chilling time)
330 kcal/1386 kJ

Black and White Cream Slices

1 Preheat the oven to 200 °C/390 °F/ gas mark 6. Make a sponge mix with the eggs, 2 tbsp tepid water, sugar, flour, cornflour, cocoa powder and salt.

2 Spread the mixture onto a baking tray lined with baking parchment and bake for about 10 minutes on the middle shelf of the oven. Remove from the oven and turn onto a kitchen towel sprinkled with sugar. Remove the parchment and allow to cool.

3 Make a vanilla cream with the milk, cornflour, egg yolk, vanilla pulp and sugar. Whisk the cream until stiff. Stir the vanilla mixture until smooth, then fold in the cream.

4 Cut the sponge through twice horizontally. Spread one base with half of the cream, then place the second base on top.

5 Spread the remaining cream on top, then cover with the third base. Leave in a cool place. Dust the sponge with icing sugar and cut into 12 slices.

Makes 12 slices

For the sponge:
4 eggs
120 g/4 ¼ oz sugar
75 g/2 ½ oz plain flour
75 g/2 ½ oz cornflour
2 tbsp cocoa powder
a pinch of salt

For the filling:
½ l/18 fl oz milk
40 g/1 ½ oz cornflour
4 egg yolks.
pulp of ½ vanilla pod
120 g/4 ¼ oz sugar
300 g/10 ½ oz whipping cream
icing sugar to dust
sugar to dust

Preparation time:
40 minutes (plus chilling time)
286 kcal/1202 kJ

Puff Pastry

Puff Pastry:

250 g/9 oz plain flour
25 g/1 oz melted butter
a pinch of salt
1 egg yolk
⅛ l (= 125 ml)/4 ½ fl oz
water
250 g/9 oz cold butter
25 g/1 oz plain flour
flour for the work surface

Cake shown
Caramel Tart
(below, recipe page 86/87)

True puff pastry is really a form of pasta but with butter. However, making it is not as easy as describing it. You need a lot of time and some practice. Alternatively you can always use ready-made frozen puff pastry. The one thing that determines the quality of your puff pastry is the consistency of the butter. This must be well chilled before working it into the pastry. Rolling it out and folding it many times results in lots of thin layers of butter between the pastry which, when baked, produces the typical leaves associated with this type of pastry.

1 Sieve 250 g/9 oz plain flour into a bowl.

2 Add 25 g/1 oz melted butter to the flour. Mix the butter with some of the flour to form a crumble.

3 Add the salt and egg yolk. Gradually add the water, mix all ingredients together well.

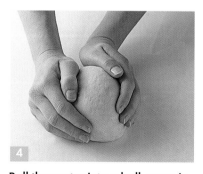

4 Roll the pastry into a ball, wrap in cling film and leave in a cool place for about 30 minutes.

Basic Recipe

5 Dice 250 g/9 oz cold butter, sieve 25 g/1 oz flour over it and mix well.

9 Fold the empty half of the pastry on top, seal the edges well.

13 Roll out the pastry again to form a square.

6 Place the butter between two layers of cling film.

10 Roll out into a rectangle.

14 Fold pastry together in three layers, leave in a cool place. Use the pastry as directed in the recipe.

7 Roll out to measure about 19 cm x 19 cm (8 in x 8 in) and allow to cool well (about 30 minutes).

11 Fold pastry to a third of its original size. Dust with flour and roll out again.

15 For bases roll out the pastry to about 3 mm (⅛ in) thick. Cut along the edge of the base of a spring-release tin.

8 Roll out pastry to measure about 20 x 40 cm (8 in x 16 in). Place the butter on top of the pastry. Brush the edges with water.

12 Fold again to make three layers of the same size. Leave in a cool place for 20–30 minutes.

16 Place the cut out base onto a baking tray rinsed with water.

Plum Tart

Makes 12 slices

150 g/5 oz puff pastry (frozen)
500 g/1 lb 2 oz plums
80 g/2 ¾ oz sugar
4 tbsp lemon juice
200 g/7 oz sponge biscuits
8 tbsp sweet sherry
100 g/3 ½ oz ground hazelnuts
sugar for dusting
butter to grease the tin
flour for the work surface

Preparation time:
45 minutes
182 kcal/767 kJ

1 Roll the puff pastry out on a well-floured work surface. Place a 20 cm/8 in pie tin on top upside down and cut round the edge to make the base.

2 Cut the remaining pastry into narrow strips. Wash and halve the plums, remove the stones. Mix with the sugar and lemon juice.

3 Crumble the sponge biscuits and add to the plums. Mix in the sherry and hazelnuts. Preheat the oven to 220 °C/430 °F/gas mark 7.

4 Grease the base of the pie tin with butter and line with the pastry. Pour in the filling. Brush the edges of the pie tin with cold water.

5 Arrange the strips of pastry decoratively on top. Then brush with cold water and sprinkle with sugar. Bake for 30 minutes on the middle shelf of the oven.

Dutch Cherry Torte

1 Preheat the oven to 220 °C/430 °F/ gas mark 7. Cut the pastry into thirds, roll out individually, then cut out three bases 24 cm/10 in across, prick several times with a fork. Place on a baking tray rinsed with cold water and bake each base for 10 minutes on the second shelf from the bottom of the oven.

2 Wash and stone the cherries, cook for a few minutes with ⅛ l/4 ½ fl oz water, the sugar and cinnamon. Thicken with the cornflour.

3 Add the vanilla essence to the cream and whip until stiff. Spread the cherry puree over one cooled base. Stir the icing sugar into the cherry brandy, spread this on top of the puree as a glaze. Allow glaze to dry.

4 Spread the cherry puree over another base, cover with ⅓ of the cream. Place the last base on top and cover with another ⅓ of the cream. Cut the glazed base into 12 slices, arrange on top of the cream.

5 Spread the remaining cream around the sides (leaving some aside for decoration), and sprinkle with the flaked almonds. Decorate the torte with whirls of cream and cherries.

Makes 12 slices

300 g/10 ½ oz puff pastry (frozen)

50 g/1 ¾ oz roasted flaked almonds

300 g/10 ½ oz cherries

30 g/1 oz sugar

¼ tsp cinnamon

15 g/½ oz cornflour

500 g/1 lb 2 oz whipping cream

2-3 drops vanilla essence

2 tbsp redcurrant jelly

100 g/3 ½ oz icing sugar

1–2 tbsp cherry brandy

cherries to decorate

Preparation time:
60 minutes
306 kcal/1285 kJ

Caramel Tart

1 Wash, peel and halve the apples, remove the cores and cut into thin slices. Sprinkle with lemon juice. Preheat the oven to 200 °C/390 °F/ gas mark 6.

2 Roll the pastry out on a well-floured work surface, cut out a base to line a 30 cm/12 in greased tart tin. Prick the base several times with a fork and sprinkle with breadcrumbs. Bake the base for about 30 minutes on the middle shelf of the oven.

3 Heat ⅛ l/4 ½ fl oz water and 75 g/2 ½ oz sugar in a large shallow pan until the sugar has dissolved completely. Add the apple slices to the sugar syrup and gently cook for about 1–2 minutes, stirring constantly. The apple slices should remain crisp and retain their shape. Finally pour off the syrup into another pan.

4 Stir the remaining sugar into the syrup. Simmer at a high temperature until the syrup has turned pale brown.

5 Arrange the fruit on the pastry. Spoon the syrup over the apples. Allow to cool, then decorate with the lemon balm.

Makes 12 slices

1 kg/2 lb 3 oz apples
2 tbsp lemon juice
250 g/9 oz puff pastry (frozen)
3 tbsp breadcrumbs
180 g/6 ½ oz sugar
lemon balm to decorate
flour for the work surface
butter to grease the tin

Preparation time:
50 minutes
286 kcal/1201 kJ

Plum Cake

Makes 12 slices

250 g/9 oz puff pastry (frozen)

150 g/5 oz white cooking chocolate

250 g/9 oz whipping cream

500 g/1 lb 2 oz plums

50 g/1 ¾ oz sugar

2 tbsp lemon juice

2 cl plum brandy

icing sugar to dust

flour for the work surface

Preparation time:
40 minutes
436 kcal/1948 kJ

1 Preheat the oven to 220 °C/430 °F/ gas mark 7. Roll out the puff pastry sheets on a floured work surface. Cut out three bases using a 26 cm/10 in spring-release baking tin. Line two baking trays with baking parchment and place the three bases on them. Bake for about 20 minutes on the middle shelf of the oven.

2 Melt the chocolate and the cream in a pan at a low temperature. Then allow to cool, and leave in a cool place.

3 Wash, dry and halve the plums, remove the stones. Briefly heat the plums with the sugar, lemon juice and plum brandy. Whisk the chocolate and cream until stiff.

4 Cover one base with half of the plums and then spread half of the cream on top. Place the next base on top, cover with the remaining plums and then with the remaining cream. Place the last base on top, press down slightly and dust with icing sugar.

Blueberry Tart

1 Defrost the pastry as instructed on the packet and roll out on a well-floured work surface to fit on a baking tray. Line the baking tray with baking parchment, then place the pastry on top. Preheat the oven to 220 °C/430 °F/gas mark 7.

2 Wash and dry the blueberries. Add half the blueberries to the crème de Cassis and lemon juice in a pan and simmer for 4–5 minutes at a low temperature. Spread the cooked blueberries over the pastry while still warm, and arrange the remaining blueberries on top.

3 Arrange flakes of butter over the blueberries and bake for 15 minutes on the middle shelf of the oven. Finally dust with icing sugar.

Makes 24 slices

250 g/9 oz puff pastry (frozen)

900 g/2 lb blueberries

50 ml/1 ¾ fl oz crème de Cassis (blackcurrant-flavoured liqueur)

3 tbsp lemon juice

100 g/3 ½ oz butter

icing sugar to dust

flour for the work surface

Preparation time:
45 minutes
105 kcal/443 kJ

Nectarine and Quark Pastries

Makes 6 slices

200 g/7 oz puff pastry (frozen)

350 g/12 oz fresh nectarines

juice and zest of ½ untreated lemon

100 g/3 ½ oz low-fat quark

2 egg yolks

2–3 drops vanilla essence

1 tbsp sugar

1 tbsp milk

flour for the work surface

icing sugar to dust

Preparation time:
50 minutes
234 kcal/986 kJ

1 Defrost the puff pastry as instructed on the packet, and roll out the sheets individually on a well-dusted work surface. Preheat the oven to 200 °C/390 °F/gas mark 6.

2 Peel the nectarines and slice. Then sprinkle with a little lemon juice.

3 Mix the quark with 1 egg yolk, vanilla essence, sugar, the remaining lemon juice and lemon peel. Pour the quark mixture into the centre of each pastry. Roll up the edges and then place some nectarine slices inside.

4 Mix the remaining egg yolk with the milk and brush over the pastries. Line a baking tray with baking parchment. Place the pastries on the baking parchment and bake for 25 minutes on the middle shelf of the oven. Dust with icing sugar before serving.

Strawberry Cream Slices

1 Preheat the oven to 220 °C/430 °F/ gas mark 7. Cut the puff pastry into 8 equal pieces and arrange on a baking tray lined with baking parchment. Prick several times with a fork, then bake for about 12 minutes on the middle shelf of the oven until the pastry rises.

2 Wash and dry the strawberries. Heat briefly with orange juice and icing sugar, then strain through a sieve. Whisk the cream and vanilla essence until stiff.

3 Cut a layer from each of the pastry slices and spread each base with apple jelly. Spread the cream over the slices and drizzle with strawberry puree. Replace the pastry lid and dust with icing sugar.

Makes 8 slices

4 sheets puff pastry (frozen)

300 g/10 ½ oz strawberries

2 tbsp orange juice

3 tbsp icing sugar

250 g/9 oz whipping cream

2–3 drops vanilla essence

2 tbsp apple jelly

icing sugar to dust

Preparation time: 60 minutes
268 kcal/1126 kJ

Redcurrant Slices

Makes 18 slices

For the pastry:
800 g/1 lb 12 oz quark
8 tbsp oil
2 eggs
200 g/7 oz sugar
400 g/14 oz plain flour
½ tsp baking powder
4 tbsp milk

For the topping:
500 g/1 lb 2 oz redcurrants
6 tbsp redcurrant jelly
2 tbsp grappa or brandy
40 g/1 ½ oz desiccated coconut
2–3 drops vanilla essence
6 tbsp lemon juice
grated zest of ½ untreated lemon
6 sheets white leaf gelatine

Preparation time:
50 minutes (plus setting time)
208 kcal/876 kJ

1 Preheat the oven to 180 °C/355 °F/ gas mark 4. Drain 300 g/10 ½ oz quark into a strainer and squeeze out gently. Add oil, eggs, 100 g/3 ½ oz sugar, flour, baking powder and milk, and mix to a smooth pastry.

2 Line a baking tray with baking parchment. Roll out the pastry onto the parchment and bake for 30 minutes on the middle shelf of the oven. Wash and dry the redcurrants.

3 Heat the redcurrant jelly with the grappa, spread over the baked base. Cover with redcurrants and coconut. Mix the remaining quark, vanilla essence, the remaining sugar, lemon juice and peel.

4 Soak the gelatine, squeeze out, then dissolve in a little tepid water and stir into the quark mixture. Spread over the cake and leave in the fridge to set.

Layered Pear Torte

1 Make a choux pastry with the flour, ¼ l/ 9 fl oz water, salt, butter and eggs. Grease the base of a 20 cm/8 in spring-release baking tin and dust with flour. Spread about 2 tbsp of the pastry thinly over the base and bake for 10 minutes at 200 °C/ 390 °F/gas mark 6 on the middle shelf of the oven. Allow to cool on a cooling rack.

2 Bake another 4 bases in the same way. Peel and core the pears, cut into thin slices. Bring the red wine to the boil with 50 g/ 1 ¾ oz sugar and the cinnamon, add the pear slices and cook for 3 minutes. Allow them to cool in the liquid.

3 Soak the gelatine in a little water. Mix the quark with the lemon juice and the rest of the sugar. Dissolve the gelatine in a little water at a low temperature.

4 Then stir into the quark. Whisk the cream until stiff and fold in. Drain the pears. Pour the quark cream into an icing bag with star nozzle. Arrange ¼ of the sliced pears on each of 4 of the bases.

5 Squeeze ¼ of the quark mixture over the pears on one base, then place the next base on top and repeat the process. Cut the fifth choux base into eight slices and arrange on top of the torte. Dust with icing sugar and decorate with swirls of pink icing (optional).

Makes 8 slices

150 g/5 oz plain flour
a pinch of salt
65 g/2 ½ oz butter
4 eggs
4 fresh pears (about 600 g/1 lb 5 oz)
½ l/18 fl oz red wine
150 g/5 oz sugar
½ stick cinnamon
4 sheets white leaf gelatine
250 g/9 oz low-fat quark
2 tbsp lemon juice
250 g/9 oz whipping cream
butter to grease the tin
flour for the work surface
icing sugar to dust

Preparation time:
1 hour 30 minutes
287 kcal/1206 kJ

Mandarin Tart

Makes 24 slices

300 g/10 ½ oz quark
8 tbsp oil
2 eggs
100 g/3 ½ oz sugar
400 g/14 oz plain flour
½ tsp baking powder
4 tbsp milk
800 g/1 lb 12 oz
mandarins (tinned)
5 egg yolks
1 tbsp cornflour
7 tbsp yoghurt
1 tsp grated zest of an
untreated lemon
5 egg whites
flour for the work surface

Preparation time:
50 minutes
181 kcal/763 kJ

1 Drain the quark in a sieve and squeeze out gently. Then mix with oil, eggs, sugar, flour, baking powder and milk to make a smooth pastry. Line a baking tray with baking parchment. Roll the pastry out on a well-floured work surface. Place the pastry onto the baking tray. Preheat the oven to 180 °C/ 355 °F/gas mark 4.

2 Drain the mandarins. Whisk the egg yolks, cornflour and yoghurt until foamy in a bowl over hot water. Add the lemon peel. Whisk the egg whites until stiff and fold into the mixture with the mandarins.

3 Spread the mixture over the pastry and bake for about 30 minutes on the middle shelf of the oven.

Quark Pastries

1 Mix the quark with the sugar, egg, salt and oil. Mix the flour with the baking powder. Sieve half of the mixture over the quark and fold in. Sieve the remaining flour over the mixture and mix to a smooth pastry. Leave to rest for about 10 minutes, then mix again.

2 For the filling mix the Mascarpone with the sugar and egg yolks. Drain the pineapple slices well, half or quarter the slices. Peel and slice the kiwis. Toss the fruit in the coconut. Preheat the oven to 200 °C/390 °F/gas mark 6.

3 Roll the pastry out into a rectangle measuring 30 x 40 cm (12 x 16 in) on a well-floured work surface and cut into 12 squares of 10 cm (4 in) each. Line a baking tray with baking parchment, place the squares on the baking parchment. Put 1 tbsp Mascarpone cream onto each square, then arrange the fruit on top.

4 Roll up the edges and press in position. Bake the quark pastries for about 20 minutes on the middle shelf of the oven.

5 Allow to cool on a cooling rack. Dust with icing sugar before serving.

Makes 12 slices

For the pastry:
150 g/5 oz low-fat quark
75 g/2 ½ oz sugar
1 egg
a pinch of salt
6 tbsp oil
250 g/9 oz plain flour
2 tsp baking powder

For the filling:
250 g/9 oz Mascarpone
70 g/2 ½ oz sugar
2 egg yolks
100 g/3 ½ oz pineapple slices (tinned)
2 kiwis
desiccated coconut for tossing
icing sugar to dust
flour for the work surface

Preparation time:
60 minutes (plus resting time)
270 kcal/1134 kJ

Muffins & Co

Blueberry Muffins

Makes 12

12 paper cases
200 g/7 oz plain flour
60 g/2 oz rolled oats
1 tsp baking powder
½ tsp bicarbonate of soda
2 eggs
180 g/6 ½ oz brown sugar
3 tsp Bourbon vanilla essence
150 g/5 oz softened butter
300 g/10 ½ oz sour cream
200 g/7 oz blueberries (frozen, not defrosted)

Preparation time:
40 minutes
783 kcal/3287 kJ

1 Mix the flour with the oats, baking powder and bicarbonate of soda. Beat the eggs, add the sugar, vanilla essence, butter and sour cream and blend. Add the flour mixture and mix well.

2 Preheat the oven to 180 °C/355 °F/ gas mark 4. Place the paper cases into a muffin tray.

3 Wash and dry the blueberries. Carefully stir into the cake mixture. Spoon the mixture into the paper cases and bake for about 25 minutes on the middle shelf of the oven until golden brown.

4 Leave the muffins on the tray to rest for five more minutes, then take out and serve warm.

Surprise Cinnamon Muffins

1 Mix the flour with the cinnamon, baking powder and bicarbonate of soda. Beat the egg. Add the sugar, oil, yoghurt and coffee and mix well. Stir in the flour mixture until all dry ingredients are moist.

2 Preheat the oven to 180 °C/355 °F/ gas mark 4. Place the paper cases in the muffin tray.

3 Spoon half of the mixture into the paper cases. Put a piece of chocolate in the middle of the mixture in each case, then cover up with the remaining mixture. Bake for 25 minutes on the middle shelf of the oven.

4 Leave the muffins to rest for another 5 minutes on the tray. Decorate with cocoa beans and serve.

Makes 12

12 paper cases
250 g/9 oz plain flour
2 tsp cinnamon
2 ½ tsp baking powder
½ tsp bicarbonate of soda
1 egg
130 g/4 ½ oz sugar
80 ml/2 ¾ fl oz vegetable oil
250 g/9 oz yoghurt
75 ml/2 ½ fl oz cold coffee
12 pieces plain chocolate
chocolate beans to decorate

Preparation time:
45 minutes
383 kcal/1602 kJ

Light Nut Muffins

Makes 12

200 g/7 oz plain flour

75 g/2 ½ oz desiccated coconut

75 g/2 ½ oz ground hazelnuts

2 ½ tsp baking powder

½ tsp bicarbonate of soda

2 eggs

125 g/4 ½ oz sugar

80 ml/2 ¾ fl oz oil

250 g/9 oz sour cream

2 tbsp rum

butter to grease the tray

cream, cashew nuts and brown sugar to decorate

Preparation time:
40 minutes
820 kcal/3444 kJ

1 Mix the flour with the coconut, nuts, baking powder and bicarbonate of soda. Beat the eggs. Add the sugar, oil, sour cream, rum, and flour mixture. Keep stirring until all the dry ingredients are moist.

2 Preheat the oven to 180 °C/355 °F/ gas mark 4. Grease the muffin tray.

3 Spoon the mixture into the muffin tray. Bake for 25 minutes on the middle shelf of the oven. Allow muffins to cool, then decorate with cream, cashew nuts and brown sugar.

Tipsy Cherry Muffins

1 Preheat the oven to 180 °C/355 °F/ gas mark 4. Grease the muffin tray and put in the fridge.

2 Mix the flour with the baking powder. Beat the butter with the sugar until creamy. Stir in eggs and yoghurt alternately. Add the flour mixture and stir until all the dry ingredients are moist.

3 Add the drained cherries and chocolate flakes. Spoon the mixture into the muffin tray and bake for about 25 minutes on the middle shelf of the oven. Remove from the oven and leave to rest in the tray for another 5 minutes.

4 Sprinkle cherry brandy over the warm muffins. Decorate with cream, cocktail cherries and chocolate flakes before serving.

Makes 12

250 g/9 oz plain flour
3 tsp baking powder
125 g/4 ½ oz butter
120 g/4 ¼ oz sugar
2 eggs
200 g/7 oz full fat yoghurt
250 g/9 oz Morello cherries (out of a jar)
50 g/1 ¾ oz chocolate flakes
5 tbsp cherry brandy
butter to grease the tray
cream, cocktail cherries, and chocolate flakes to decorate

Preparation time:
45 minutes
750 kcal/3150 kJ

Banana Coconut Muffins

Makes 12

12 paper cases
230 g/8 oz plain flour
80 g/2 ¾ oz desiccated coconut
2 ½ tsp baking powder
½ tsp bicarbonate of soda
a pinch of salt
125 g/4 ½ oz low-fat margarine
1 egg
50 g/1 ¾ oz sweetener
175 g/6 oz puréed bananas
75 ml/2 ½ fl oz buttermilk
low-fat yoghurt, bananas, desiccated coconut and lemon balm to decorate

Preparation time:
45 minutes
553 kcal/2321 kJ

1 Preheat the oven to 180 °C/355 °F/ gas mark 4. Put the paper cases into the muffin tray.

2 Mix the flour with the desiccated coconut, baking powder, bicarbonate of soda and salt. Melt the margarine. Beat the egg. Stir in the margarine, sweetener, puréed banana and buttermilk. Fold in the flour mixture and stir until all dry ingredients are moist.

3 Spoon the mixture into the paper cases and bake for about 25 minutes on the middle shelf of the oven. Leave the muffins to rest in the tray for about 5 minutes.

4 Remove from the oven, allow to cool and decorate with yoghurt, banana slices and coconut. Decorate with a few leaves of lemon balm before serving.

Pineapple Muffins

1 Preheat the oven to 180 °C/355 °F/ gas mark 4. Grease the muffin tray and put in the fridge.

2 Drain the diced pineapple in a sieve, then sprinkle with rum and a little juice. Leave a few pieces aside.

3 Mix the flour with the coconut, baking powder and bicarbonate of soda. Beat the egg. Stir the sugar, oil, yoghurt and pineapple into the egg. Add the flour mixture and stir until all dry ingredients are moist.

4 Spoon the mixture into the tray and bake for 20 minutes on the middle shelf of the oven. Remove from the oven and allow to rest for 5 minutes.

5 Remove the muffins from the tray and allow to cool. Stir the chocolate strands into the cream. Decorate the muffins with the chocolate cream, diced pineapple and lemon balm.

Makes 12

150 g/5 oz diced pineapple (tinned)

3 tbsp rum

50 ml/1 ¾ fl oz pineapple juice

250 g/9 oz plain flour

50 g/1 ¾ oz desiccated coconut

2 tsp baking powder

½ tsp bicarbonate of soda

1 egg

125 g/4 ½ oz sugar

80 ml/2 ¾ fl oz vegetable oil

200 g/7 oz thick pineapple yoghurt

butter to grease the tray

cream, chocolate strands and lemon balm to decorate

Preparation time:
45 minutes
593 kcal/2488 kJ

Black-and-White Muffins

Makes 12

12 paper cases
270 g/10 oz plain flour
3 tsp baking powder
½ tsp bicarbonate of soda
2 eggs
175 g/6 oz sugar
100 ml/3 ½ fl oz
vegetable oil
280 ml/10 fl oz buttermilk
2–3 drops vanilla essence
25 g/1 oz chocolate
blancmange powder
60 ml/2 fl oz milk
125 g/4 ½ oz whipping
cream
chocolate sticks (white
and dark chocolate), and
cocoa powder to
decorate

Preparation time:
45 minutes
1028 kcal/4316 kJ

1 Preheat the oven to 180 °C/355 °F/ gas mark 4. Put the paper cases in the muffin tray.

2 Mix 200 g/7 oz flour with 2 tsp baking powder and the bicarbonate of soda. Beat one egg. Mix with 140 g/5 oz sugar, 80 ml/2 ¾ fl oz oil and the buttermilk. Add the flour and stir until all the dry ingredients are moist.

3 Spoon the mixture into the muffin cases. For the dark chocolate mixture mix 70 g/2 ½ oz flour with ½ tsp baking powder, some vanilla essence and the chocolate blancmange powder. Beat one egg, add 35 g/1 oz sugar, 20 ml/4 tsp oil and 60 ml/2 fl oz milk and stir well. Add the flour mixture and mix well.

4 Spoon the dark mixture into the middle of the light mixture. Bake for 25 minutes on the middle shelf of the oven. Remove from the oven and leave to rest in the tray for another 5 minutes.

5 Decorate with whirls of whipped cream, white and dark chocolate sticks and cocoa powder and serve.

Chocolate and Blackberry Muffins

1 Preheat the oven to 180 °C/355 °F/ gas mark 4. Grease the muffin tray. Mix the flour with the baking powder, bicarbonate of soda and cocoa powder.

2 Beat the egg. Stir in the sugar, oil, 250 g/ 9 oz yoghurt and the flour mixture until all dry ingredients are moist.

3 Spoon the mixture evenly into the muffin tray and bake for 25 minutes on the middle shelf of the oven. Allow the muffins to rest and cool for 5 minutes.

4 Stir the remaining yoghurt with the vanilla essence until smooth.

5 Remove the stalks, wash and dry the blackberries. Decorate the muffins with the yoghurt cream and blackberries and serve.

Makes 12

250 g/9 oz plain flour
2 ½ tsp baking powder
½ tsp bicarbonate of soda
2 tbsp cocoa powder
1 egg
120 g/4 ¼ oz sugar
80 ml/2 ¾ fl oz oil
350 g/12 oz yoghurt
2–3 drops vanilla essence
100 g/3 ½ oz blackberries
butter to grease the tray

Preparation time:
40 minutes
573 kcal/2405 kJ

Brandy Bagels

Makes 20

250 ml/9 fl oz milk
50 g/1 ¾ oz butter
1 tsp salt
1 tbsp sugar
20 g/ ¾ oz yeast
1 egg (separated)
400 g/14 oz plain flour
400 g/14 oz whipping cream
20 g/ ¾ oz icing sugar
2 tbsp brandy
grated chocolate (flakes)
flour for the work surface

Preparation time:
35 minutes (plus resting time)
790 kcal/3318 kJ

1 Bring the milk to the boil with the butter, salt and sugar, stirring constantly. Allow to cool for a while, then crumble in the yeast. Allow to stand for about 10 minutes.

2 Beat the egg white and stir into the yeast milk mixture. Gradually add the flour and knead. Knead everything to a smooth dough until it no longer sticks to your hands. Cover and leave for 1 hour in a warm place to rise.

3 Preheat the oven to 200°C/390°F/gas mark 6. Boil a panful of water. Make the pastry into balls and press a hole in the centre with your index finger, to form a ring.

Pre-cook the bagels for about 1 minute in the boiling water, a few at a time. Remove from the water, drain and brush with egg yolk.

4 Put the bagels on the baking tray and bake for about 15 minutes on the middle shelf of the oven. Remove from the oven and allow to cool.

5 Whisk the cream, icing sugar and brandy until stiff. Cut the bagels in half and fill with the brandy cream. Put the halves back together and decorate with the remaining cream and grated chocolate.

Strawberry Bagels

1 Heat the milk until tepid, crumble in the yeast and stir. Add the oil, 1 tbsp sugar and 2 pinches of salt and stir well. Cover and leave for 15 minutes in a warm place to rise.

2 Add the flour and 1 egg and make into a smooth dough. Cover and leave for another 40 minutes in a warm place to rise.

3 Knead the dough and divide into 8 pieces. Roll each into a ball and press a hole in the centre, forming a ring. Leave for another 20 minutes to rise.

4 Preheat the oven to 200 °C/390 °F/gas mark 6 and line a baking tray with baking parchment. Bring the remaining sugar to the boil with 3 litres of water. Cook 2 bagels at a time in this water for 2 minutes on either side. Leave to drain on a cooling rack.

5 Place the bagels on the baking tray, brush with egg and bake for 25 minutes on the middle shelf of the oven.

6 Remove the stalks, wash and dry the strawberries, then slice. Blend the bananas and stir with the Mascarpone and rum to make a smooth cream.

7 Cut the cooled bagels in half and fill with the cream mixture. Arrange the strawberries on top. Put the bagels back together and decorate with cream mixture, strawberries and icing sugar.

Makes 8

⅛ l/4 ½ fl oz milk
20 g/¾ oz yeast
25 ml/1 fl oz oil
3 tbsp sugar
2 pinches salt
300 g/10 ½ oz plain flour
1 egg
1 egg yolk
200 g/7 oz strawberries
150 g/5 oz bananas
500 g/1 lb 2 oz Mascarpone
2 tbsp rum
icing sugar to dust

Preparation time:
45 minutes (plus resting time)
793 kcal/3329 kJ

Blackberry Doughnuts

Makes 12

500 g/1 lb 2 oz plain flour

1 packet dried yeast

80 g/2 ¾ oz sugar

a pinch of salt

1 egg

½ l/18 fl oz tepid milk

50 g/1 ¾ oz butter

4 tbsp blackberry jam

2 tbsp blackberry liqueur

1 egg white

flour for the work surface

clarified butter for the deep fryer

icing sugar to dust

Preparation time:
30 minutes (plus resting time)
352 kcal/1479 kJ

1 Mix the flour with the dried yeast, sugar and salt in a bowl. Separate the egg. Add the egg yolk, milk and butter and knead to make a smooth dough.

2 Cover the dough and allow to rise until it has doubled in size. Then roll out about 1 cm/½ in thick on a well-floured work surface.

3 Mix the jam with the liqueur. With a cup about 8 cm/3 ¼ in across cut 24 rounds of out the dough and fill half of them with 2 tsp of the filling.

4 Brush the edges with egg white and place the remaining (empty) rounds on top. Press the edges together well and leave to rise for another 30 minutes. Heat the clarified butter in a pan or chip pan to 180 °C/355 °F.

5 Fry a few of the doughnuts at a time in the hot clarified butter for about 10 minutes. Turn once after five minutes. Drain the doughnuts on kitchen paper, then dust with icing sugar.

Kiwi Custard Donuts

1 Heat the oil in the deep fryer. Mix the flour with the baking powder, sugar, nutmeg and salt. Mix the butter well with the egg, milk and vanilla essence. Add the flour mixture and mix together well.

2 Roll out the pastry on the well-floured work surface to about 1 cm/½ in thick. Cut out donuts using a doughnut cutter or two glasses of different sizes.

3 Fry the donuts for about 3 minutes on either side in the hot oil, remove and drain on kitchen paper.

4 Peel the kiwis, halve and slice. Squeeze the custard into the centre of the donuts using an icing bag. Decorate with kiwi slices and icing sugar and serve.

Makes 24

630 g/1 lb 6 oz plain flour

1 ½ tsp baking powder

200 g/7 oz sugar

1 tsp nutmeg

½ tsp salt

2 tbsp melted butter

1 egg

300 ml/10 ½ fl oz milk

2–3 drops vanilla essence

2 kiwis

custard (ready-made)

vegetable oil for the deep fryer

flour for the work surface

icing sugar to dust

Preparation time:
25 minutes
900 kcal/3780 kJ

MUFFINS & CO

Mango Horns

Makes 4

250 g/9 oz plain flour

250 g/9 oz cold butter

250 g/9 oz ground almonds

½ tsp sugar

orange zest

3 mangos

4 tbsp almond liqueur

1 tbsp lemon juice

200 g/7 oz blackberries

3 tbsp brown sugar

2 tbsp maple syrup

flour for the work surface

2 egg yolks to brush

Preparation time:
60 minutes (plus resting time)
764 kcal/3208 kJ

1 Mix the flour with the butter, almonds sugar and orange zest to a smooth pastry and leave for about 15 minutes to rest.

2 Peel the mangos, remove the stones and dice the flesh. Sprinkle with almond liqueur and lemon juice and leave to soak for about 5 minutes.

3 Wash the blackberries, blend and add to the diced mangos with the sugar and maple syrup. Mix well.

4 Preheat the oven to 180 °C/355 °F/ gas mark 4. Roll the pastry out on a well-floured work surface and cut into squares of about 10 x 10 cm (4 x 4 in).

5 Spread the fruit on the squares and roll up from one corner, making horns. Brush with egg yolk and bake for about 18 minutes on the middle shelf of the oven.

Strawberry Iced Buns

1 Heat the milk in a pan. Sieve the flour into a bowl, make a well, crumble the yeast into the well. Pour in the milk. Knead well and leave for about 20 minutes in a warm place to rise.

2 Mix the butter with the sugar, salt, egg and 1 egg yolk into the dough and knead. Roll into a ball, cover and leave to rise until it has doubled in size. Preheat the oven to 180 °C/355 °F/gas mark 4.

3 Wash and dry the strawberries, then slice. Sprinkle with desiccated coconut and gin.

4 Knead the dough once more and roll out. Cut out circles about 12 cm/4 ¾ in across. Put 1 tbsp of strawberries onto each. Brush the edges with milk, fold and press together. Brush the buns with milk and 1 egg yolk, then bake for about 20 minutes on the middle shelf of the oven.

5 Mix the icing sugar with the lemon juice and melted butter. Brush over the buns before serving.

Makes 24

160 ml/5 fl oz (= ¼ pint) milk
400 g/14 oz plain flour
30 g/1 oz fresh yeast
60 g/2 oz butter
40 g/1 ½ oz sugar
a pinch of salt
1 egg
2 egg yolks
400 g/14 oz strawberries
80 g/2 ¾ oz desiccated coconut
100 ml/3 ½ fl oz gin
100 g/3 ½ oz icing sugar
1 tbsp lemon juice
10 g/⅓ oz melted butter
milk to brush
flour for the work surface

Preparation time:
45 minutes
95 kcal/401 kJ

Savouries

Leek and Onion Tart

Makes 12

200 g/7 oz plain flour
100 g/3 ½ oz butter
1 egg yolk
salt
500 g/1 lb 2 oz leeks
50 g/1 ¾ oz onions
2 tbsp oil
100 g/3 ½ oz raw smoked ham
125 g/4 ½ oz sour cream
3 eggs
salt
pepper
50 g/1 ¾ oz grated Emmental cheese
pulses or beans to bake blind
butter for the tin

Preparation time:
45 minutes (plus cooling time)
330 kcal/1380 kJ

1 Mix the flour, butter, egg yolk, salt and 3 tbsp water into a smooth pastry. Roll out and place into a greased spring-release baking tin, making the sides 3 cm/1 ¼ in high. Put in a cool place for about 30 minutes.

2 Finely slice the leeks, dice the onions and braise them for a few minutes in oil. Dice the ham very finely and mix in. Preheat the oven to 200 °C/390 °F/gas mark 6.

3 Mix the sour cream with the eggs, salt and pepper. Line the pastry base in the tin with baking parchment, cover with pulses or beans and bake blind for about 10 minutes.

4 Remove the pulses and baking parchment. Spread the leek and onion mixture onto the base.

5 Pour the egg and cream mixture on top and sprinkle with Emmental cheese. Bake for about 20 minutes until the egg and cream mixture has set.

with Smoked Ham

Tomato Flan

Makes 18

300 g/10 ½ oz plain flour
200 g/7 oz butter flakes
a pinch of salt
¼ tsp grated lemon peel
1 egg
700 g/1 lb 9 oz plum tomatoes
250 g/9 oz soft goat's cheese
3 tbsp capers
3 spring onions
salt
freshly ground pepper
1 sprig rosemary
3 cloves of garlic
100 g grated Gruyère cheese

Preparation time:
50 minutes (plus cooling time)
160 kcal/647 kJ

1 Mix the flour with the flaked butter, salt, lemon peel and egg on a work surface until very fine. Then make the pastry into a ball, wrap in cling film and leave for about 1 hour in the fridge.

2 Preheat the oven to 200 °C/390 °F/ gas mark 6. Remove the stalks from the tomatoes, wash and slice.

3 Mix the goat's cheese with the capers. Prepare and wash the spring onions, cut into rings and stir into the cheese mixture. Line a baking tray with baking parchment, place the rolled-out pastry on top of this. Cover with the cheese mixture.

4 Arrange the tomatoes on top, season with salt and pepper. Wash and dry the rosemary, remove the individual needles. Peel the cloves of garlic and cut into thin slices.

5 Arrange the rosemary and garlic on the tomatoes. Sprinkle the Gruyère cheese on top and bake for about 25 minutes on the middle shelf of the oven.

Onion Tart

1 Make a short crust pastry with the flour, 100 g butter, salt and 3 tbsp cold water. Wrap the pastry in cling film and leave for about 30 minutes to chill in the fridge.

2 Preheat the oven to 175 °C/345 °F/ gas mark 3 ½. Roll the pastry out thinly and line a spring-release baking tin with it. Prick several times with a fork and bake for about 10 minutes on the middle shelf of the oven.

3 For the filling peel the onions and cut into thin rings. Remove the rind from the bacon, dice finely.

4 Heat the remaining butter in a large frying pan and fry the bacon lightly. Then add the onions and fry until golden brown, turning constantly.

5 Season to taste with caraway seeds, salt and pepper. Grate the raclette and Emmental cheese coarsely. Mix the sour cream with the eggs and cornflour. Pour the onion mixture onto the base, and the egg mixture on top. Sprinkle with the cheese. Bake for about 30 minutes on the middle shelf of the oven, until the surface turns golden brown. Serve immediately.

Makes 12

200 g/7 oz plain flour
130 g/4 ½ oz butter
¾ tsp salt
1 kg/2 lb 3 oz large onions
200 g/7 oz smoked lean bacon
1 tsp caraway seeds
salt
pepper
250 g/9 oz raclette cheese
200 g/7 oz Emmental cheese
200 g/7 oz sour cream
3 eggs
1 tbsp cornflour

Preparation time:
55 minutes (plus cooling time)
458 kcal/1924 kJ

117

Cheese Bagels

Makes 8

500 g/1 lb 2 oz plain flour

½ cube fresh yeast

1 ½ tsp salt

1 egg yolk

80 g grated Emmental cheese

40 g/1 ½ oz sunflower seeds

flour for the work surface

Preparation time:
40 minutes (plus resting time)
573 kcal/2405 kJ

1 Sieve the flour into a bowl. Make a well at the centre, crumble in the yeast and add 340 ml/12 fl oz tepid water to the yeast. Let the yeast dissolve and mix well. Cover and leave for about 15 minutes to rise.

2 Mix in the salt and knead the mixture to a smooth dough. Cover and leave to rise for another 30 minutes. Preheat the oven to 225 °C/440 °F/gas mark 7, and boil a large panful of water.

3 Knead the dough thoroughly on a well-floured work surface. Make into 8 balls and press a large hole in the middle of each. Flatten the bagels slightly, then allow to rest for 5 minutes.

4 Put the bagels in the boiling water for about 30 seconds. Remove from the water, drain and place on a baking tray lined with baking parchment.

5 Beat the egg yolk and brush over the bagels. Sprinkle cheese and sunflower seeds over the bagels, then bake for about 25 minutes on the middle shelf of the oven.

Potato and Cheese Cookies

1 Heat 200 ml/7 fl oz water in a pan with the butter. Stir in the oats and the eggs, and continue stirring until the mixture comes away from the edge of the pan. Remove from the heat.

2 Dice the ham finely, mash the potatoes and add to the pastry with the ham. Season to taste with salt and pepper. Allow the pastry to rest for about 30 minutes in the fridge.

3 Preheat the oven to 200 °C/390 °F/ gas mark 6. Line a baking tray with baking parchment. Make the dough into small balls, press flat and arrange on the baking tray, leaving enough space in between each one.

4 Sprinkle the cheese on the cookies and bake for about 15 minutes on the middle shelf of the oven.

Makes 18

60 g/2 oz butter
120 g/4 ¼ oz rolled oats
3 eggs
100 g/3 ½ oz ham
250 g/9 oz boiled potatoes
pepper
salt
100 g/3 ½ oz grated cheese

Preparation time:
35 minutes (plus resting time)
370 kcal/1554 kJ

Spicy Cheese Sticks

Makes 24

200 g/7 oz puff pastry
2 eggs
200 g/7 oz grated
Emmental cheese
1 bunch basil
a pinch of salt
freshly ground pepper
paprika powder
sesame and coarse salt
to garnish
flour for the work surface

Preparation time:
40 minutes
223 kcal/936 kJ

1 Roll out the puff pastry on a well-floured work surface and brush with the beaten egg.

2 Put the cheese into a bowl and mix with the remaining egg. Wash and dry the basil, chop into small pieces, stir into the cheese mixture, then season to taste with salt, pepper and paprika.

3 Preheat the oven to 200 °C/390 °F/ gas mark 6. Cut the pastry into strips and cover half of them with the cheese mixture. Place the remaining pastry strips on top and press together lightly.

4 Twist the pastry strips and arrange evenly on a baking tray lined with baking parchment. Sprinkle with sesame and coarse salt. Then bake for about 10 minutes on the middle shelf of the oven.

Paprika Flan

1 Heat the milk in a pan. Sieve the flour into a bowl, make a well in the middle and crumble the yeast into the well. Pour in the milk. Knead well and leave for about 20 minutes in a warm place to rise.

2 Add the butter, sugar, salt, 1 egg and egg yolk. Knead again and roll into a ball, cover and leave to rise until double in size. Preheat the oven to 200 °C/390 °F/ gas mark 6.

3 Prepare the peppers, wash and cut into strips. Heat the herb butter in a pan and sauté the strips of pepper in this. Peel the cloves of garlic and squeeze through a garlic press into the mixture. Drain the olives and add to the mixture.

4 Roll out the dough on a well-floured work surface, then place onto a baking tray lined with baking parchment. Arrange the pepper strips over the dough. Beat the remaining eggs, add the cheese and salt, then pour over the pepper strips. Bake for about 25 minutes on the middle shelf of the oven.

Makes 24 slices

160 ml/5 fl oz (= ¼ pint) milk
400 g/14 oz wholegrain wheat flour
30 g/1 oz fresh yeast
60 g/2 oz butter
40 g/1 ½ oz sugar
a pinch of salt
4 eggs
1 egg yolk
200 g/7 oz red peppers
200 g/7 oz yellow peppers
2 tbsp herb butter
2 cloves of garlic
80 g/2 ¾ oz black olives
100 g/3 ½ oz grated Emmental cheese
flour for the work surface

Preparation time:
50 minutes (plus resting time)
144 kcal/605 kJ

Spelt and Lemon Bread

Makes 24 slices

160 ml/5 fl oz (= ¼ pint) milk

400 g/14 oz spelt flour or wholemeal flour

30 g/1 oz fresh yeast

110 g/4 oz butter

120 g/4 ¼ oz sugar

a pinch of salt

1 egg

1 egg yolk

100 g/3 ½ oz candied lemon peel

50 g/1 ¾ oz raisins

80 g/2 ¾ oz cashew nuts

grated zest of 2 untreated lemons

flour for the work surface

coarse sugar to dust

Preparation time:
50 minutes (plus resting time)
151 kcal/638 kJ

1 Heat the milk in a pan. Sieve the flour into a bowl, make a well at the centre and crumble in the yeast. Pour in the milk, then knead. Leave for about 20 minutes in a warm place to rise. Preheat the oven to 200 °C/ 390 °F/gas mark 6.

2 Add 60 g/2 oz butter, 40 g/1 ½ oz sugar, salt, egg, egg yolk, candied lemon peel, raisins and nuts. Knead and make into a ball, then cover and allow to rise until it has doubled in size.

3 Knead the lemon zest into the dough, then make into a long roll shape on a well-floured work surface. Place on a baking tray lined with baking parchment.

4 Bake the spelt and lemon bread for 20 minutes on the middle shelf of the oven. Sprinkle with coarse sugar before serving.

Caraway and Herb Rolls

1 Heat the milk in a pan. Sieve the flour into a bowl, make a well at the centre and crumble in the yeast. Pour in the milk, then knead. Leave for about 20 minutes in a warm place to rise.

2 Add butter, sugar, salt, egg and egg yolk. Knead and roll into a ball, cover and leave to rise until it has doubled in size.

3 Preheat the oven to 200 °C/390 °F/ gas mark 6. Add the caraway seeds, linseed, sunflower seeds and herbs to the dough and knead. Leave to rise for another 5 minutes.

4 Shape the dough into small loaves and make diagonal cuts with a knife on the top. Line a baking tray with baking parchment, then arrange the rolls on the baking parchment. Bake for about 30 minutes on the middle shelf of the oven.

Makes 24

160 ml/5 fl oz (= ¼ pint) milk
400 g/14 oz rye flour
30 g/1 oz fresh yeast
60 g/2 oz butter
40 g/1 ½ oz sugar
a pinch of salt
1 egg
1 egg yolk
1 tsp caraway seeds
1 tsp linseed
1 tsp sunflower seeds
100 g/3 ½ oz mixed herbs
(frozen or freshly chopped)

Preparation time:
50 minutes (plus resting time)
97 kcal/407 kJ

123

Nutty Roll Ring

Makes 24

160 ml/5 fl oz (= ¼ pint) milk

400 g/14 oz plain flour

30 g/1 oz fresh yeast

60 g/2 oz butter

40 g/1 ½ oz sugar

a pinch of salt

1 egg

1 egg yolk

20 ml/4 tsp Arrak or brandy

120 g/4 ¼ oz linseed

1 tsp turmeric

120 g/4 ¼ oz coarsely chopped pecan nuts

100 g/3 ½ oz grated carrots

100 g/3 ½ oz chopped almonds

100 g/3 ½ oz chopped walnuts

flour for the work surface

Preparation time:
45 minutes (plus resting time)
212 kcal/891 kJ

1 Heat the milk in a pan. Sieve the flour into a bowl, make a well at the centre and crumble in the yeast. Pour in the milk. Knead and leave for about 20 minutes in a warm place to rise.

2 Add the butter, sugar, salt, egg and egg yolk. Knead and roll into a ball, cover and leave to rise until the dough has doubled in size.

3 Preheat the oven to 200 °C/390 °F/ gas mark 6. Divide the dough into 4 portions. Add the arrak and linseed to the first portion, the turmeric and chopped pecan nuts to the second, the chopped almonds and grated carrots to the third, and the chopped walnuts to the last. Knead and leave to rise for another 10 minutes.

4 Roll the portions out on a well-floured work surface and make into several rolls. Arrange the rolls in a spiral shape on a baking tray lined with baking parchment, then bake for 25 minutes on the middle shelf of the oven.

Puff Pastry Cheese Pretzels

1 Lay the blocks of puff pastry next to each other and defrost as stated on the packet. Preheat the oven to 200 °C/390 °F/gas mark 6.

2 Place the pastry blocks on a lightly floured work surface, sprinkle with cheese and roll out to form rectangles measuring about 24 x 15 cm/10 x 6 in. Cut lengthwise into strips.

3 Shape the strips of pastry into small pretzels, brush with the beaten egg yolk, then sprinkle with poppy seeds, sesame seeds, coarse salt and caraway seeds. Bake for about 15 minutes on the second shelf from the bottom of the oven.

Makes 16

450 g/1 lb puff pastry (frozen)

150 g/5 oz grated Emmental cheese

1 egg yolk

poppy seeds, sesame seeds, coarse salt and caraway seeds to garnish

flour for the work surface

Preparation time:
25 minutes
185 kcal/717 kJ

Biscuits & Co

Whities with Limes

Makes 16

200 g/7 oz plain flour

4 tsp baking powder

100 g/3 ½ oz quark or soft cheese

1 tbsp milk

4 tbsp oil

60 g/2 oz brown sugar

2–3 drops vanilla essence

50 g/1 ¾ oz icing sugar

2 tsp lime juice

lime zest to decorate

Preparation time:
30 minutes
355 kcal/1491 kJ

1 Preheat the oven to 180 °C/355 °F/ gas mark 4. Line a baking tray measuring about 30 x 20 cm/ 12 x 8 in with baking parchment.

2 Mix the flour with the baking powder. Mix the quark with the milk, oil and sugar until creamy. Gradually stir in the flour mixture.

3 Spread the mixture on the baking tray and bake for about 15 minutes. Cut into 16 pieces while still hot.

4 Mix the lime juice with the icing sugar and stir until smooth. Brush over the whities, decorate with zest of lime, and serve.

Vanilla Fingers

1 Whisk the butter with the sugar, vanilla and salt until creamy. Add the egg and continue whisking until the sugar is completely dissolved. Stir in the milk. Preheat the oven to 200 °C/390 °F/gas mark 6.

2 Mix the flour with the baking powder, sieve and fold into the mixture. Pour the mixture into a piping bag with a hole nozzle.

3 Squeeze the mixture out into finger-length strips about 5–8 cm/2–3 in long onto a baking tray lined with baking parchment, leaving adequate space between each.

4 Bake for about 15 minutes on the middle shelf of the oven.

Makes 50

200 g/7 oz butter
160 g/5 ½ oz sugar
pulp of 1 vanilla pod
a pinch of salt
1 egg
4 tbsp milk
280 g/10 oz plain flour
1 tsp baking powder

Preparation time:
45 minutes
32 kcal/134 kJ

Cranberry Diamonds

1 Let the cranberries start defrosting, leaving some aside to decorate. Preheat the oven to 180 °C/355 °F/gas mark 4. Grease the baking tray.

2 Melt the butter with the cocoa and sugar, stirring constantly until the sugar is dissolved. Mix the flour with the baking powder and add to the butter mixture. Stir in the eggs, then the cranberries.

3 Spread the mixture onto the baking tray. Mix the crème fraîche with the sugar, vanilla essence, butter, and flour, and spread on top of the mixture. Sprinkle with chocolate.

4 Bake for about 40 minutes on the middle shelf of the oven. Allow to cool on the tray. Cut into diamonds and decorate with cream and cranberries.

Variations

1 Raspberry diamonds: make the diamonds as given in the basic recipe, but use raspberries.

2 Nut and cream diamonds: make the diamonds as given in the basic recipe. Cut out large diamond-shaped biscuits. Crumble the remaining mixture, brown in a frying pan with chopped nuts, allow to cool and stir into the whipped cream. Use as filling between 2 biscuits.

3 Walnut diamonds: make the diamonds as given in the basic recipe. Stir walnut crunch into the whipped cream. Decorate with dots of cream and walnuts, and dust with chocolate.

4 Egg liqueur and cream diamonds: make the diamonds as given in the basic recipe, decorate with whipped cream and egg liqueur, and dust with cocoa powder.

Makes 12

100 g/3 ½ oz cranberries (frozen)
120 g/4 ¼ oz butter
4 tbsp cocoa powder
200 g/7 oz brown sugar
150 g/5 oz plain flour
1 heaped tsp baking powder
2 eggs
150 ml/5 fl oz (= ¼ pint) crème fraîche
75 g/2 ½ oz sugar
2–3 drops vanilla essence
50 g/1 ¾ oz softened butter
1 egg
2 tbsp plain flour
50 g/1 ¾ oz flaked chocolate
butter for the tin
whipping cream to decorate

Preparation time:
55 minutes
985 kcal/4137 kJ

Nut Cookies

Makes 45

280 g/10 oz plain chocolate
280 g/10 oz plain flour
1 tsp baking powder
½ tsp salt
90 g/3 oz softened butter
210 g/7 ½ oz sugar
3 eggs
2–3 drops vanilla essence
45 cashew nuts
icing sugar to dust

Preparation time:
40 minutes
100 kcal/418 kJ

1 Preheat the oven to 160 °C/320 °F/ gas mark 2–3. Line a baking tray with baking parchment. Break the chocolate into a metal bowl, melt over hot water and remove from the heat.

2 Mix the flour with the baking powder and salt. Cream the butter, gradually adding the sugar and vanilla essence. Add the eggs one at a time, stir well.

3 Add the cooled melted chocolate to the mixture. Gradually fold in the flour until the mixture is smooth.

4 Make the mixture into balls 3 cm/ 1 ¼ in across and arrange on the baking tray each 5 cm/2 in apart. Press a cashew nut into the centre of each.

5 Bake for about 12 minutes on the middle shelf of the oven. Dust the cookies with icing sugar before serving.

Black and White Biscuits

1 Separate the eggs. Whisk the egg yolk with the salt and sugar until creamy. Wash the lemon, grate the zest and squeeze out the juice. Stir both into the egg yolk mixture. Preheat the oven to 200 °C/ 390 °F/gas mark 6.

2 Whisk the egg white until stiff, add to the egg yolk mixture. Mix the flour with the cornflour and sieve over the egg white. Fold in carefully.

3 Line a baking tray with baking parchment, and spoon the mixture onto the baking parchment 1 tbsp at a time, ensuring there is space for the biscuits to increase in size. Make into round biscuit shapes with a spoon.

4 Bake for about 10 minutes on the middle shelf of the oven. Remove from the paper and allow to cool on a cooling rack. Melt the plain and nut chocolate together, and dip half of each biscuits into this mixture.

Makes 30

4 eggs
a pinch of salt
100 g/3 ½ oz sugar
1 untreated lemon
75 g/2 ½ oz plain flour
75 g/2 ½ oz cornflour
100 g/3 ½ oz plain chocolate
100 g/3 ½ oz nut chocolate

Preparation time:
30 minutes
73 kcal/308 kJ

133

Spiced Slices

Makes 24

60 g/2 oz candied lemon

60 g/2 oz candied orange

60 g/2 oz raisins

5 tbsp Armagnac (brandy)

150 g wheat flour

150 g/5 oz wholegrain spelt flour

200 g/7 oz butter (cut in pieces)

170 g/6 oz icing sugar

a pinch of salt

½ tsp grated zest of 1 untreated lemon

1 egg

1 tsp nutmeg

1 tsp ground cardamom

1 tsp ground allspice

2 tsp ground cinnamon

100 g/3 ½ oz maple syrup

4 tbsp cognac

Preparation time:
50 minutes (plus cooling time)
171 kcal/720 kJ

1 Chop the candied lemon, orange and raisins coarsely, heat in a pan with the Armagnac and leave to soak for about 15 minutes.

2 Mix the flour in a bowl with the butter, 70 g/ 2 ½ oz icing sugar, salt, lemon zest and egg.

3 Finally add the spices and Armagnac fruit mixture and mix well. Roll the mixture into a ball, wrap in cling film and leave for about 1 hour in the fridge.

4 Preheat the oven to 200 °C/390 °F/gas mark 6. Roll out the mixture on a baking tray lined with baking parchment and bake for 30 minutes on the middle shelf of the oven.

5 Heat the syrup with the cognac and stir in the remaining icing sugar.

6 Remove the cake from the oven and brush with the cognac mixture.

Walnut Rounds

Makes 30

200 g/7 oz softened butter

160 g/5 ½ oz sugar

2 tbsp orange flower water

250 g/9 oz plain flour (sieved)

60 g/2 oz chopped walnuts

1 tsp cinnamon

butter for the tray

Preparation time:
50 minutes
330 kcal/1386 kJ

1 Preheat the oven to 160 °C/320 °F/ gas mark 2–3. Grease a baking tray with the melted butter. Whisk butter and 100 g/3 ½ oz sugar in a small bowl until creamy.

2 Pour the mixture into a large bowl and stir in the orange flower water and flour with a metal spoon. Use your hands to make a firm mixture.

3 For the filling mix the walnuts, the remaining sugar and cinnamon carefully in a bowl. To make each biscuit, take 1 rounded tbsp mixture and roll into a ball, press your thumb into the centre to form a hollow. Spoon 1 tsp filling into this.

4 Arrange the biscuits on a baking tray and press slightly to flatten. Bake for about 20 minutes in the oven until they are golden brown. Allow to cool on a cooling rack, then serve.

Yoghurt Cups

1 Preheat the oven to 200 °C/390 °F/ gas mark 6. Mix the butter well with the icing sugar, egg white and flour. Line a baking tray with baking parchment.

2 Roll out the mixture on a well-floured work surface and cut out circles 10 cm/ 4 in across using a pastry cutter. Bake these for 6 minutes on the middle shelf of the oven.

3 Allow the cups to cool slightly, then brush with the chocolate glaze. Make up the red wine cream as stated on the packet. Fold in the pear juice and yoghurt, allow the cream mixture to set in the fridge.

4 Pour the cream mixture into a piping bag and pipe evenly into the cups. Decorate with almond sticks or flakes, then serve.

Makes 4

50 g/1 ¾ oz butter
50 g/1 ¾ oz icing sugar
1 egg white
50 g/1 ¾ oz plain flour
100 g/3 ½ oz plain cooking chocolate for the glaze
300 g/10 ½ oz red wine cream (ready-made)
5 tbsp pear juice
125 g/4 ½ oz yoghurt
1 tbsp almond sticks
flour for the work surface

Preparation time:
25 minutes (plus cooling)
443 kcal/1855 kJ

Marzipan Cookies

1 Preheat the oven to 190 °C/375 °F/ gas mark 5. Line a baking tray with baking parchment. Whisk the butter with the sugar until creamy. Stir in the egg, then mix in the flour. Roll out the mixture about 5 cm/ 2 in thick on a well-floured work surface. Then cut out circles 8 cm/3 ¼ in across.

2 Put half of the circles on the baking tray, with a piece of marzipan at the centre. Sprinkle grated chocolate on top. Then cover with the other half of the circles.

3 Press the edges of the filled biscuits together well and bake for about 12 minutes on the middle shelf of the oven. When cool, decorate with white glaze.

Makes 12

150 g/5 oz butter
150 g/5 oz brown sugar
1 egg
250 g/9 oz plain flour
100 g/3 ½ oz marzipan
100 g/3 ½ oz grated chocolate
80 g/2 ¾ oz white cooking chocolate for the glaze
flour for the work surface

Preparation time:
45 minutes
930 kcal/3906 kJ

Variations

1 Marzipan hearts: cut out heart shapes, using the basic recipe above. For the filling use marzipan and small cubes of apricot. Brush with apricot jam if wanted, and decorate with white and dark chocolate.

2 Cocoa cookies: dust the cookies with cocoa powder and decorate with lines of white chocolate.

3 Pistachio cookies: make the cookies according to the basic recipe, dip half of each cookie in white chocolate, and sprinkle with chopped pistachios.

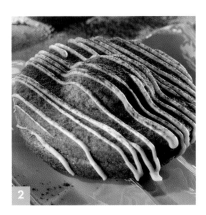

Orange and Lemon Rounds

Makes 40

125 g/4 ½ oz butter

125 g/4 ½ oz sugar

1 egg

200 g/7 oz plain flour

1 tsp baking powder

1 pinch of salt

1 untreated lemon

2 tbsp orange marmalade

1 tbsp orange juice

4 mandarins

lemon zest and icing
sugar to decorate

butter for the baking tray

Preparation time:
25 minutes
57 kcal/239 kJ

1 Preheat the oven to 200 °C/390 °F/ gas mark 6. Grease the baking tray. Whisk the butter with the sugar until creamy. Stir in the egg. Mix the flour with the baking powder and salt, and add to the butter mixture. Make into a smooth mixture.

2 Wash the lemon and grate the zest. Press out the juice and leave aside. Add the zest to the mixture. Make the mixture into about 40 small balls, arrange on the baking tray and press down a little to flatten. Bake for 12 minutes on the middle shelf of the oven.

3 Remove the cookies from the oven and allow to cool. Mix the orange marmalade with a little orange juice until smooth. Peel the mandarins and separate out the segments. Decorate the cookies with marmalade, mandarin segments and lemon zest, then dust with icing sugar before serving.

Filled Coconut Cubes

1 Preheat the oven to 180°C/355°F/ gas mark 4. Line the baking tray with baking parchment. Chop up the white chocolate very finely. Separate the eggs. Whisk the butter, sugar and egg yolk until smooth and creamy. Stir in the flour, white chocolate, desiccated coconut (leave 2 tbsp of coconut aside), and the vanilla essence. Whisk the egg whites until stiff and fold in.

2 Spread the mixture on the baking tray and bake for 15 minutes on the middle shelf of the oven.

3 Allow the mixture to cool, then cut through horizontally. Heat the jam or jelly and brush over the bottom half. Place the other layer on top and press together. Cut into cubes measuring 4 x 4 cm/1 ½ x 1 ½ in and decorate with dark chocolate and the remaining desiccated coconut.

Makes 12

50 g/1 ¾ oz white cooking chocolate

2 eggs

100 g/3 ½ oz softened butter

75 g/2 ½ oz sugar

50 g/1 ¾ oz plain flour

200 g/7 oz desiccated coconut

2–3 drops vanilla essence

250 g quince jelly or apricot jam

50 g plain cooking chocolate

2 tbsp desiccated coconut

Preparation time: 45 minutes
813 kcal/3413 kJ

141

Christmas

Winter Apple Cake

Makes 24 slices

300 g/10 ½ oz plain flour
200 g/7 oz butter (flaked)
100 g/3 ½ oz sugar
a pinch of salt
¼ tsp grated zest of an untreated lemon
1 egg
1 tsp mixed spice
500 g/1 lb 2 oz apples
3 tbsp lemon juice
25 g/1 oz chopped chocolate
25 g/1 oz currants
50 g/1 ¾ oz ground almonds
1 tbsp rum
4 tbsp orange juice
100 g/3 ½ oz marzipan
50 g/1 ¾ oz icing sugar
200 g/7 oz cooking chocolate
icing sugar to dust
flour for the work surface

Preparation time:
50 minutes (plus cooling time)
212 kcal/890 kJ

1 Mix the flour, flakes of butter, sugar, salt, zest of the lemon, egg and mixed spices well on a work surface. Then shape into a ball. Wrap in cling film and leave for about 1 hour in a cool place. Preheat the oven to 200 °C/390 °F/gas mark 6.

2 Peel and halve the apples, remove the cores, then dice. Sprinkle with lemon juice and add to the mixture together with the chopped chocolate, currants, almonds and rum.

3 Roll the pastry out on a baking tray lined with baking parchment. Bake for about 10 minutes on the middle shelf of the oven.

4 Knead the marzipan, orange juice and icing sugar and roll out on a lightly floured work surface. Cut out stars of assorted sizes.

5 Melt the cooking chocolate in a bowl over hot water and use to decorate the cake. Decorate with the marzipan stars and dust with icing sugar.

Santa Claus Cake

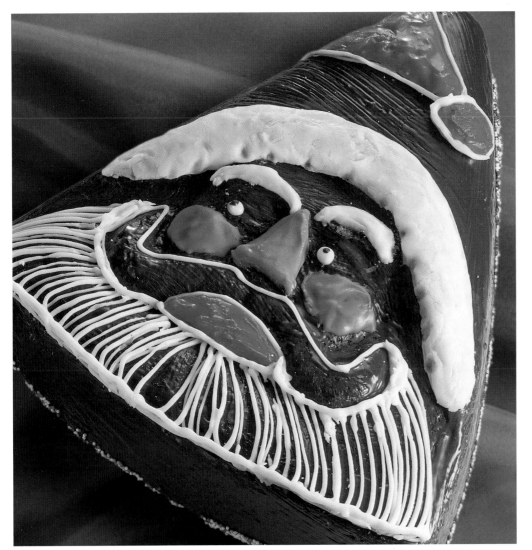

Makes 1 cake

6 eggs
200 g/7 oz butter
250 g/9 oz sugar
125 g/4 ½ oz plain flour
2 tsp baking powder
2 tsp cinnamon
250 g/9 oz ground
hazelnuts
200 g/7 oz chocolate
leaves
200 g/7 oz plain cooking
chocolate
100 g/3 ½ oz icing sugar
4–5 tbsp hot water
various food colourings
butter and breadcrumbs
for the mould

Preparation time:
1 hour 30 minutes
7400 kcal/30900 kJ

1 Preheat the oven to 175 °C/345 °F/ gas mark 3 ½. Separate the eggs. Beat the butter until creamy. Add 150 g/5 oz sugar and beat until the sugar is dissolved. Then gradually add the separated egg yolks. Whisk the remaining sugar with the egg white until stiff. Whisk ⅓ of the egg white into the egg yolk mixture.

2 Mix the flour, baking powder and cinnamon, sieve over the egg mixture and carefully fold in. Then fold in the remaining egg white, together with the ground hazelnuts and chocolate leaves.

3 Grease a Santa Claus- shaped baking mould (2 l/3 ¾ pints), and sprinkle with breadcrumbs. Pour in the cake mixture,

spread evenly and bake for 60 minutes on the middle shelf of the oven. When done, allow the cake to cool for about 5 minutes in the mould, then carefully turn onto a cooling rack and allow to cool completely.

4 Melt the cooking chocolate in a bowl over warm water. Coat the cake with the chocolate. Stir the icing sugar with enough water to form a smooth, thick icing. Take small portions of the icing and add food colouring as required. Pour the icing into small piping bags made with baking parchment and decorate the cake.

Dresden Christmas Stollen

Makes 30 slices

175 g/6 oz peeled almonds
175 g/6 oz sultanas
100 g/3 ½ oz currants
100 g/3 ½ oz finely diced candied lemon peel
100 g/3 ½ oz finely diced candied orange peel
2–3 drops vanilla essence
grated zest of 1 untreated lemon
3 tbsp rum
500 g/1 lb 2 oz plain flour
60 g/2 oz fresh yeast
90 g/3 oz sugar
⅛ l/4 ½ fl oz tepid milk
a pinch of salt
250 g/9 oz butter
flour for the work surface
150 g/5 oz melted butter to glaze
100 g/3 ½ oz icing sugar to dust

Preparation time:
40 minutes (plus resting time)
277 kcal/1160 kJ

1 Grind half of the almonds, chop the remaining ones coarsely. Mix with sultanas, currants, lemon and orange peel, vanilla essence, lemon zest and rum, cover and leave to stand overnight.

2 Sieve the flour into a bowl, make a well at the centre and crumble the yeast into the well. Sprinkle a little sugar over the yeast, pour in the tepid milk and dissolve the yeast. Arrange the salt and flaked butter around the edge of the flour, then knead everything working from the middle towards the sides using the dough hooks of the mixer.

3 Cover and leave in a warm place until the mixture has doubled in size. Then mix in the prepared fruits.

4 Roll out the dough on a well-floured work surface to form a rectangle about 40 x 30 cm / 15 x 12 in. Brush with water. Fold together along the long side so that the end overlaps slightly. Press the roll flat with a kitchen roll, making it into a stollen shape. Put the stollen on a baking tray lined with baking parchment. Cover and leave for about another 20 minutes to rise. Preheat the oven to 200 °C/390 °F/gas mark 6.

5 Bake the stollen for 40 minutes on the middle shelf of the oven. Brush with melted butter while still hot, then dust with the icing sugar. Repeat until both butter and icing sugar have been used up. Wrap the stollen in aluminium foil and leave for at least 3 weeks to mature.

Layer Cake

Makes 16 slices

250 g/9 oz butter

250 g/9 oz sugar

2–3 drops vanilla essence

2 eggs

4 egg yolks

100 g/3 ½ oz cornflour

1 tsp baking powder

150 g/5 oz plain flour

4 egg whites

2 tbsp apricot jam

200 g/7 oz plain cooking chocolate

butter for the tin

flour for the work surface

Preparation time:
2 hours
334 kcal/1405 kJ

1 Preheat the oven to 200 °C/390 °F/ gas mark 6. Whisk butter, sugar and vanilla essence until creamy. Gradually add the eggs and egg yolks and continue whisking. Mix the cornflour with the baking powder and flour, then stir in, a spoonful at a time.

2 Whisk the egg white until stiff, then fold into the mixture. Grease a 16 cm/6–7 in spring-release baking tin and dust with flour. Spoon 1 tbsp mixture into the tin and spread thinly. Bake for about 4 minutes on the top shelf of the oven. Spoon in another 1 tbsp mixture, spread and bake. Repeat until the tin has been filled to the top.

3 Turn the cake onto the greased base of a larger spring-release tin and bake for a short time on the middle shelf of the oven until golden brown. Make 2 more cakes in the same way.

4 Heat the apricot jam and pass through a strainer. Use to assemble the cakes on top of each other. Melt the chocolate, then brush over the entire cake.

Christmas Angel

1 Sieve the flour into a bowl, make a well at the centre and crumble the yeast into the well. Sprinkle a little sugar over it, pour in the tepid milk and dissolve the yeast.

2 Put the remaining sugar, flaked butter, salt and cardamom around the edge of the flour and knead everything together to make a smooth dough, working from the middle towards the sides. Cover and leave for about 40 minutes in a warm place to rise.

3 Preheat the oven to 200 °C/390 °F/ gas mark 6. Roll the dough out on a greased baking tray to about 5 cm/2 in thick. With a home-made cardboard angel template, cut out the angel (about 25 cm/ 10 in length). Mix the egg with a little milk and brush the angel with this mixture. Decorate with hazelnuts and raisins. Bake for 20 minutes on the middle shelf of the oven. Leave on the tray to cool.

4 For the glaze mix the icing sugar with enough egg white to form a thick, smooth mixture. Add food colouring if wanted. Pour small quantities of coloured mixture into small piping bags and decorate the angel.

Makes 1 angel

250 g/9 oz plain flour
15 g/½ oz fresh yeast
40 g/1 ½ oz sugar
⅛ l/4 ½ fl oz tepid milk
40 g/1 ½ oz butter
a pinch of salt
¼ tsp cardamom
1 egg
milk to glaze
almonds, hazelnuts and raisins
150 g/5 oz icing sugar
about ½ egg white
food colouring
butter to grease the tray

Preparation time:
50 minutes (plus resting time)
2145 kcal/9009 kJ

Dominoes

1 Whisk the butter until creamy. Add the sugar and vanilla and whisk until the sugar has dissolved. Gradually stir in the eggs. Mix the flour with the cocoa powder and baking powder and sieve. Add the walnuts to the egg and butter mixture and fold into the flour mixture.

2 Preheat the oven to 175 °C/345 °F/ gas mark 3 ½. Line a baking tray with baking parchment. Make raised edges round the parchment, forming a rectangle 40 x 20 cm / about 15 x 8 in. Spread the mixture onto this. Bake for 15 minutes on the second tray from the bottom. Remove from the baking tray by lifting the baking parchment and allow to cool on a cooling rack.

3 Mix the marzipan with the icing sugar and raspberry brandy. Remove the cake from the baking parchment and cut in half to make two even squares. Roll out the marzipan between two layers of cling film to fit one of the cake squares.

4 Spread raspberry jam onto one of the cake squares. Place the layer of marzipan on top, cover this with raspberry jam, then place the second square of cake on top. Put the whole cake onto a tray and place another tray with two weights (e.g. two tins of food) on top. Leave for about 3–4 hours in a cool place.

5 With a wet knife trim the edges of the cake to make them even. Finally cut the cake into 49 cubes (7 x 7).

6 Melt the chocolate and glaze over warm water and mix well. Dip half of the dominoes completely in the glaze, tap any excess off on the edge of the bowl, allow to cool on aluminium foil.

7 Melt the white chocolate and coconut oil over warm water and mix well. Dip the remaining dominoes completely in the glaze. Tap any excess glaze off on the edge of the bowl, allow to cool on aluminium foil.

Makes 49 pieces

For the mixture:
125 g/4 ½ oz butter
160 g/5 ½ oz brown sugar
pulp of 1 vanilla pod
2 eggs
65 g/2 ½ oz plain flour
50 g/1 ¾ oz cocoa powder
½ tsp baking powder
100 g/3 ½ oz ground walnuts

For the filling:
100 g/3 ½ oz marzipan
30 g/1 oz icing sugar
1 tbsp raspberry brandy
150 g/5 oz raspberry jam

For the coating:
200 g/7 oz plain cooking chocolate
200 g/7 oz dark cake glaze
400 g/14 oz white cooking chocolate
80 g/2 ¾ oz coconut oil

Preparation time:
60 minutes (plus cooling time)
183 kcal/765 kJ

CHRISTMAS

Star Cake

Makes 12 slices

8 egg whites

300 g/10 ½ oz sugar

grated zest of 1 untreated lemon

2–3 drops vanilla essence

8 egg yolks

6 cooking apples

250 g/9 oz ground poppy seeds

200 g/7 oz ground nuts

50 g/1 ¾ oz plain flour

butter to grease the tin

icing sugar to dust

Preparation time:
1 hour 30 minutes
58 kcal/1503 kJ

1 Whisk the egg whites with 8 tbsp cold water until very stiff. Add the sugar, grated lemon zest and vanilla essence. Stir in the egg yolk. Preheat the oven to 200 °C/ 390 °F/gas mark 6.

2 Peel and core the apples, cut into cubes and stir into the egg mixture. Carefully stir in the ground poppy seeds, nuts and flour.

3 Grease a 28 cm/11 in spring-release baking tin, then line with baking parchment. Pour in the cake mixture and bake for 60 minutes on the bottom shelf of the oven.

4 When the cake has cooled, make a star template and use to decorate with dusted icing sugar.

Viennese Biscuits

1 Beat the butter until creamy. Add the sugar, vanilla essence, vanilla and lemon zest and whisk until the sugar is dissolved. Gradually add the eggs, then stir in the almonds and fold in the sieved flour.

2 Grease the baking trays lightly and dust with flour. Spoon the mixture into a piping bag with a large star nozzle and pipe the mixture onto the baking tray, making strips about 6 cm/2 ½ in long. Leave for about 1 hour in a cool place.

3 Preheat the oven to 200 °C/390 °F/ gas mark 6. Bake for about 15 minutes on the middle shelf of the oven. Allow to cool on a cooling rack.

4 Heat the chocolate. Dip each biscuit in the chocolate to a depth of about 2 cm. Leave to set.

Makes 70

125 g/4 1/2 oz butter
250 g/9 oz sugar
2–3 drops vanilla essence
pulp of ½ vanilla pod
grated zest of an untreated lemon
2 eggs
125 g/4 ½ oz ground almonds
350 g/12 oz flour
butter and flour for the baking tray
200 g dark cooking chocolate for the glaze

Preparation time:
1 hour 15 minutes
(plus chilling time)
57 kcal/239 kJ

153

Sweet Chestnut Torte

Makes 12 slices

For the mixture:
100 g/3 ½ oz plain flour
30 g/1 oz cocoa powder
100 g/3 ½ oz plain cooking chocolate
pulp of 1 vanilla pod
20 g instant coffee powder
5 egg yolks
175 g/6 oz icing sugar
1 tbsp water
5 egg whites
a pinch of salt

For the filling:
½ l/18 fl oz milk
40 g/1 ½ oz cornflour
4 egg yolks
130 g/4 ½ oz sugar
a pinch of salt
1 vanilla pod
sugar to dust
250 g/9 oz chestnut purée (tinned)
4 tbsp rum (40%)
2 tbsp cocoa powder
125 g/4 ½ oz softened butter

To decorate:
12 fresh sweet chestnuts
oil
150 g/5 oz icing sugar
100 g/3 ½ oz milk chocolate flakes

Preparation time:
1 hour 20 minutes
498 kcal/2080 kJ

1 Mix the flour with the cocoa powder, the finely grated chocolate, the pulp from the vanilla pod and the coffee powder. Preheat the oven to 175 °C/345 °F/gas mark 3 ½.

2 Whisk the egg yolks for 6–7 minutes with 100 g/3 ½ oz icing sugar and water. Whisk the egg white, salt and remaining icing sugar until stiff. Carefully fold in the egg white, egg yolk and flour mixture to make a smooth sponge cake mixture.

3 Line the base of a 24 cm/10 in spring-release baking tin. Pour the mixture in and bake for 40 minutes on the second shelf from the bottom. Allow to cool in the tin.

4 Mix ⅛ l/4 ½ fl oz of the milk with the cornflour, egg yolk, 40 g/1 ½ oz sugar and salt. Bring the remaining milk to the boil with the remaining sugar and the vanilla pulp and vanilla pod. Remove the vanilla pod. Mix the cornflour with some milk and whisk into the boiling mixture. Simmer briefly, stirring constantly. When cool pour through a very fine sieve.

5 Pour the sweet chestnut purée through a very fine sieve, mix with rum and cocoa powder. Beat the butter until creamy, gradually stir in the chestnut purée and vanilla cream. Remove the cooled sponge base from the tin and cut through twice horizontally. Assemble the torte as follows: sponge base, ⅓ of the butter cream, sponge base, ⅓ of the butter cream, sponge mix. Spread the remaining butter cream over the entire cake.

6 To decorate make a cross with a sharp knife on the inside of the chestnuts, place on a baking tray and roast in a preheated oven at 225 °C/440 °F/gas mark 7 until they crack open. Remove the chestnuts from their shells.

7 Brush a piece of baking parchment with oil. Melt the icing sugar at a medium temperature, stirring constantly until it forms a golden brown caramel. With a fork, dip the chestnuts into the hot caramel, one at a time, until they are completely covered. Place on the oiled parchment and allow to cool. Place the chestnuts around the torte with the flaked chocolate at the centre.

Macaroons

Makes 30

3 egg whites
125 g/4 ½ oz sugar
125 g/4 ½ oz ground almonds
15 g/ ½ oz plain flour
50 g/1 ¾ oz coarsely chopped almonds
100 g/3 ½ oz apricot jam
100 g/3 ½ oz plain cooking chocolate

Preparation time:
50 minutes
78 kcal/330 kJ

1 Whisk the egg white with 100 g/3 ½ oz sugar until stiff. Mix the remaining sugar with the ground almonds and flour and fold in. Preheat the oven to 170 °C/340 °F/ gas mark 3.

2 Pour the mixture into a piping bag with a hole nozzle and pipe onto a baking tray lined with baking parchment, making a variety of shapes. Sprinkle with chopped almonds. Bake for about 20 minutes on the middle shelf of the oven.

3 Remove from the oven and allow to cool. Strain the apricot jam. Brush the smooth side of half of the macaroons with the jam.

4 Place the other half of the macaroons on top. Melt the cooking chocolate and pour into a small piping bag. Use to decorate the macaroons. Serve.

Prickly Log

1 Grate the rusk very finely. Beat the butter and sugar until creamy. Gradually add the eggs and whisk until the sugar is dissolved. Preheat the oven to 180 °C/355 °F/ gas mark 4.

2 Mix the grated almonds with the flour and baking powder, then gradually stir into the egg mixture. Finely grate 100 g/3 ½ oz chocolate. Add to the mixture together with the rum.

3 Pour the mixture into a greased semi-circular loaf tin and bake for 55 minutes on the bottom shelf of the oven.

4 Leave the log to cool for a short time in the tin, then turn out and leave to cool. For the glaze, melt 100 g chocolate with the coconut oil and cover the log with this mixture. Decorate with the almond sticks.

Makes 18 slices

125 g/4 ½ oz rusk
100 g/3 ½ oz butter
150 g sugar
4 eggs
100 g/3 ½ oz grated almonds
2 tbsp plain flour
2 tsp baking powder
200 g/7 oz plain chocolate
2 tbsp rum
25 g/1 oz coconut oil
50 g/1 ¾ oz almond sticks
butter for the tin
flour to dust

Preparation time:
1 hour 30 minutes
208 kcal/873 kJ

Crunchy Lemon Torte

1 Heat the icing sugar at a medium temperature until it turns a light brown caramel colour. Stir in the almonds. Pour the crunchy mixture onto a greased baking tray and allow to cool. Break into pieces, put into a freezer bag and crush well with a rolling pin. Preheat the oven to 175 °C/ 345 °F/gas mark 3 ½.

2 Beat the eggs, the egg yolks, sugar, salt, lemon zest and peel for 8–10 minutes in a pan over water on the highest setting until thick and creamy. Then beat for 3–4 minutes on a medium setting until cold. Melt the butter. Mix the flour and the cornflour, sieve and mix with the crunchy mixture. First fold the flour and crunchy mixture into the egg mixture, then add the butter.

3 Line a 24 cm/10 in spring-release baking tin with baking parchment. Pour in the mixture and bake for about 40 minutes on the second shelf from the bottom. Allow the base to cool in the tin.

4 To make the filling grate the limes and lemons thinly and squeeze out the juice. Mix 100 ml/3 ½ fl oz juice and the zest with the white wine. Mix ⅛ l/4 ½ fl oz of this with egg yolk, cornflour and 20 g/ ¾ oz sugar. Stir 80 g/2 ¾ oz sugar into the remaining white wine mixture and bring to the boil. Mix the cornflour with some water and whisk into the mixture, briefly allowing it to boil. Pour through a fine strainer.

5 Whisk the softened butter with a hand mixer until creamy, gradually add the lemon cream. Whisk the egg whites and the remaining sugar until stiff, then fold into the cream mixture.

6 When cool, remove the base from the tin and cut through horizontally twice. Spread two layers first with lemon marmalade, then with butter cream, and place one on top of the other. Place the third layer on top. Remove 5 tbsp of the remaining cream, pour into a piping bag with a small nozzle and put in the fridge. Cover the torte with the remaining cream mixture. Press pine nuts into position around the sides of the torte.

7 To make the glaze stir the icing sugar, lemon zest and juice, egg white and food colouring until smooth. With a palette knife spread on top of the torte, then leave for about 1 hour to dry. With a star-shaped biscuit cutter make stars and pipe the cream mixture a around the outlines of the stars. Spread some lemon marmalade into the centre of each star.

Makes 12 slices

For the mixture:
50 g/1 ¾ oz icing sugar
50 g/1 ¾ oz chopped almonds
oil
4 eggs
2 egg yolks
120 g/4 ¼ oz sugar
a pinch of salt
1 tsp grated zest of an untreated lemon
2 tbsp water
50 g/1 ¾ oz butter
100 g/3 ½ oz plain flour
50 g/1 ¾ oz cornflour

For the filling:
2 untreated limes
1 untreated lemon
¼ l/9 fl oz dry white wine
4 egg yolks
40 g/1 ½ oz cornflour
150 g/5 oz sugar
250 g/9 oz butter
2 egg whites
150 g/5 oz lemon marmalade

To decorate:
100 g/3 ½ oz roast pine nuts

For the glaze:
120 g/4 ¼ oz icing sugar
1 tsp grated zest of an untreated lemon
1 tbsp lemon juice
½ egg white
yellow food colouring
3 tbsp lemon marmalade

Preparation time:
60 minutes
585 kcal/2445 kJ

Recipe Index